A. Levasseur

To
Dick Sanders.
from
Louis Armstrong
LOUIS ARMSTRONG
Satchmo

Natalia Ewakowa

Holiday on Ice

60 Jahre – Träume auf dem Eis
60 Years – Dreams on Ice

aus dem Deutschen übersetzt
von Jon Shelton

vgs

Inhalt
Contents

Vorwort
Foreword

Die Stage Holding gehört zu den führenden Live- Entertainment-Produzenten der Welt. Das Unternehmen besteht aus einer Gruppe von Firmen, die Musicals, Eisshows, Theaterstücke, Konzerte und Veranstaltungen produzieren. In mehreren Ländern betreibt die Stage Holding eigene Spielstätten, dazu Call Center für den Ticketvertrieb.

Ende der 90er Jahre hatten wir die einmalige Gelegenheit, unsere Live-Entertainment-Aktivitäten mit HOLIDAY ON ICE zu erweitern. HOLIDAY ON ICE blickt auf eine beeindruckende, mehrere Jahrzehnte umfassende internationale Geschichte zurück und hat weltweit Millionen überaus loyaler Zuschauer. Während der letzten 7 Jahre hat HOLIDAY ON ICE alle seine Produktionen nach einem modernen, ganzheitlichen Konzept entwickelt: So sind aufregende und spektakuläre Shows entstanden, die gut bei den vielen treuen Fans ankommen und darüber hinaus ein neues Publikum anziehen.

HOLIDAY ON ICE ist ohne Zweifel internationaler Marktführer und stellt zugleich die weltgrößte Tourneeproduktion im Eis-Entertainment. Pro Jahr erleben etwa 5 Millionen Menschen eine von 3 Shows auf Tour – jede mit bis zu 50 Eistänzern und circa 350 Kostümen. Die Produktionen – ausgestattet mit eigenen mobilen Eisflächen, Licht- und Tontechnik – präsentieren sich ihren Zuschauern jährlich in insgesamt etwa 1700 Vorstellungen in 120 Städten. Im Jahr 2002 begrüßte HOLIDAY ON ICE seinen 300-millionsten Besucher: Ein beinahe unglaublicher Rekord in der Unterhaltungsbranche!

Stage Holding is one of the leading live entertainment companies in the world. It consists of a group of enterprises producing musicals, ice shows, theatre plays, concerts and events. It also runs theatres in a number of countries and organizes ticket sales through its own call centres.

In the late 90's we had a unique opportunity to acquire HOLIDAY ON ICE as an extension of our live entertainment activities. HOLIDAY ON ICE has an impressive international history of several decades combined with tremendously loyal audiences of many millions worldwide. Over the last 7 years HOLIDAY ON ICE has adopted a modern, total-show concept to its new productions, creating exciting spectacular shows that appeal to its huge fan base and at the same time attract new audiences.

HOLIDAY ON ICE is the undisputed worldwide market leader in ice entertainment and the world's largest touring ice entertainment show. Each year, an average of 5 million people come to one of the 3 shows on tour. With each show featuring up to 50 skaters, 350 costumes, their own ice floors, light and sound equipment, together they visit 120 cities worldwide each year, staging approximately 1,700 separate performances. In 2002 HOLIDAY ON ICE welcomed its 300 millionth visitor, a unique record in the world of entertainment!

In diesem farbenprächtigen Bildband zum 60. Geburtstag von HOLIDAY ON ICE werden Sie auf jene Künstler treffen, die von den Anfängen bis heute zum unglaublichen Erfolg von HOLIDAY ON ICE beigetragen haben. Werfen Sie einen exklusiven Blick hinter die Kulissen: Beeindruckende Fotografien und spannende Geschichten aus den letzten 6 Jahrzehnten lassen die besondere Atmosphäre dieser außergewöhnlichen Show für Sie lebendig werden.

Wir hoffen, diese Jubiläumsausgabe gefällt Ihnen und freuen uns darauf, Sie bei einer unserer neuen spektakulären Shows rund um den Globus zu treffen!!

In this colourful 60th anniversary book you can meet the skaters from the past and the present who have made HOLIDAY ON ICE into such an enormous success. Take an exclusive look behind the scenes where you can enjoy the energy and excitement of this extraordinary show through the amazing photographs and stories of the last 6 decades.

We hope you enjoy this special 60th anniversary edition and look forward to meeting you somewhere around the world at one of our new spectacular shows!

Joop van den Ende

Chairman of the Board

Stage Holding B.V.

Wie alles anfing
How it all started

1943

Die Weihnachtsferien geben HOLIDAY ON ICE seinen Namen: Premiere ist am 25. Dezember in Toledo, Ohio. Möglich wird mobiles Eis-Entertainment mit der Erfindung transportabler Kältesysteme aus Rohren und Kompressoren.

The Christmas season gives HOLIDAY ON ICE its name, the première is on December 25th in Toledo, Ohio. Mobile ice entertainment becomes a reality with the invention of a transportable cooling system composed of tubing and compressors.

Im Laufe seiner 60-jährigen Geschichte ist HOLIDAY ON ICE zu einem Synonym für spektakuläre Eisrevue geworden. Dabei hat alles, wie so oft, viel kleiner angefangen – genauer gesagt bei den so genannten Tank-Shows in den 30er Jahren. Das damals neuartige Kabarett auf dem Eis verdankte seinen Namen einem System aus Rohren und Kompressoren, mit dem das Eis hergestellt und das in überdimensionalen Tanks transportiert wurde. Die Shows, die in großen Hotels und Nachtclubs präsentiert wurden, erwiesen sich als wahre Publikumsmagneten. Schon bald waren mehr als 30 solcher Tank-Shows in den USA unterwegs.

Die Organisatoren einer dieser Shows im St. Regis-Hotel in Chicago, Carl Snyder und Donn Arden, waren vom Eis-Kabarett so begeistert, dass sie sich entschlossen, eine eigene Produktion ins Leben zu

In the course of its 60 year history HOLIDAY ON ICE has become the synonym for ›spectacular ice skating revue‹. But as is often the case, everything started out much smaller, to be specific it started with the so-called ›Tank Shows‹ of the 30's. This ›new‹ ice cabaret got its name from the fact that ice was first produced using a system of tubing and compressors and then transported in gigantic tanks. The shows, which played in hotels and nightclubs soon began pulling in large crowds. Soon over 30 such ›Tank Shows‹ were touring the USA.

The organizers of one such show in the St. Regis Hotel of Chicago were so excited by the ice cabaret that they decided to create a production of their own. Carl Snyder and Donn Arden opened their show on December 25th, 1943 in Toledo, Ohio. Referring to the week between Christmas and New

1943-1953

Nach Tourneen durch Amerika lässt HOLIDAY ON ICE ab 1950 auch die Herzen der Zuschauer in Europa schmelzen: Erste Stationen in Deutschland sind Frankfurt und Dortmund; die großen HOLIDAY ON ICE-Stars sind Ria Baran und Paul Falk, Weltmeister und Olympiasieger im Eiskunstlauf.

In 1950 after tours in America HOLIDAY ON ICE melts the hearts of fans in Europe. The first stops in Germany are Frankfurt and Dortmund. The big stars of HOLIDAY ON ICE are the world and Olympic figure skating champions Ria Baran and Paul Falk.

rufen. Premiere war am 25. Dezember 1943 in Toledo, Ohio. Der Name stand in Anlehnung an die freie Woche zwischen Weihnachten und Neujahr, die ›Holiday Season‹, schnell fest: HOLIDAY ON ICE!

In ihrem ersten Jahr machte die Show in acht Städten halt. Ermutigt durch die große Resonanz, präsentierten Snyder und Arden sie im Jahr danach erneut. Währenddessen träumten zwei Brüder, Emery und Calvin Gilbert aus Milwaukee, davon, eine Eis-Show zu kreieren, die mit ihrer eigenen mobilen Eisbahn auf Tour gehen konnte. Die bis dahin üblichen transportablen Eisflächen maßen nur wenige Meter – entsprechend begrenzt waren die Zuschauerkapazitäten. Doch Emery traute sich zu, eine große mobile Eisfläche zu entwerfen. Als die Gilberts 1944 von HOLIDAY ON ICE hörten, wussten sie, dass sie damit die Show-Truppe gefunden hatten, nach der sie suchten. Auf der Stelle verkauften sie ihr florierendes Lebensmittelunternehmen, schlossen sich mit Carl Snyder zusammen und investierten in die dritte HOLIDAY ON ICE-Tour, die 1945 stattfinden sollte.

Year's Day known as the ›Holiday Season‹ the production was called HOLIDAY ON ICE!

In its first year the show toured eight cities. Encouraged by the popularity of the show Snyder and Arden presented it again the following year. At the same time two brothers from Milwaukee, Emery and Calvin Gilbert, were dreaming of creating an ice show to tour with their own transportable ice rink. The transportable ice rinks of the time had a surface of only a few square feet, and thus there was not much room for an audience. Emery eventually designed a larger mobile ice rink, and in 1944 when the Gilberts heard about HOLIDAY ON ICE they knew they had found the show team that they had been looking for. They immediately sold their booming grocery store, joined up with Carl Snyder and invested in the third HOLIDAY ON ICE tour of 1945.

The show was an absolute success. However the fact that it took a lot of time to put up and to take down meant that every change of venue cost the

1953-1963

Stationiert bei der US Army In Frankfurt, besucht Elvis Presley 1958 begeistert HOLIDAY ON ICE. Später gibt die Show als erstes westliches Projekt des Kulturaustauschs zwischen den USA und der damaligen Sowjetunion ein 8 Wochen lang ausverkauftes Gastspiel in Moskau.

Stationed with the US Army in Frankfurt in 1958, Elvis Presley was an enthusiastic HOLIDAY ON ICE fan. Later the show is the first western project to visit Moscow in a cultural exchange programme between the USA and the Soviet Union, it plays for 8 sold out weeks in the Russian capital.

1963-1973

Teil des großen Erfolgs der Produktion *Gypsy Dolly* ist 1965 das deutsche Eis-Traumpaar Marika Kilius und Hans-Jürgen Bäumler. 1969 ist HOLIDAY ON ICE die Attraktion auf der Weltausstellung in Jakarta (Indonesien).

The German dream pair Marika Kilius and Hans-Jürgen Bäumler play a major role in the hugely successful production *Gypsy Dolly* in 1965. In 1969 HOLIDAY ON ICE is THE attraction at the World's Fair in Jakarta (Indonesia).

1973-1983

HOLIDAY ON ICE wird in Amsterdam (Niederlande) ansässig und gründet eine europäische Produktionsgesellschaft mit Sitz in Bern (Schweiz). 1983 erhält die Show in der Londoner Wembley Arena mit Lady Diana königlichen Besuch.

HOLIDAY ON ICE finds a home in Amsterdam (Netherlands) and founds the European Production Company in Bern (Switzerland). In 1983 at Wembley Arena in London HOLIDAY ON ICE receives a royal visit from Lady Diana.

1983-1993

Zur 750-Jahrfeier Ost-Berlins läuft Katarina Witt in 27 ausverkauften Vorstellungen im Friedrichstadt-Palast. 1988 begrüßt die Show ihren 250-millionsten Besucher und findet Eingang ins Guinnessbuch der Rekorde.

Katarina Witt skates in 27 sold out shows at the Friedrichstadt Palast for the 750th anniversary celebration of East Berlin. In 1988 the show greets its 250 millionth visitor and takes its place in the Guiness Book of World Records.

In den 50er Jahren trat HOLIDAY ON ICE in Spanien trotz mediterraner Hitze in riesigen Stierkampfarenen auf.

In the 50's HOLIDAY ON ICE performed in enormous Spanish bull fighting arenas despite Mediterranean temperatures.

Die Show wurde ein voller Erfolg. Da ihr Auf- und Abbau jedoch viel Zeit in Anspruch nahm, gingen bei jedem Ortswechsel die Einnahmen einer ganzen Woche verloren. Die Show war nicht rentabel – es sei denn mit zusätzlichen Kompressoren und Tanks, die einen fliegenden Wechsel von Stadt zu Stadt ermöglichten. Dafür aber brauchte man Geld – viel Geld. Es floss durch Morris D. Chalfen.

Chalfen, ein wohlhabender Geschäftsmann, war regelrecht besessen vom Eiskunstlauf. Als er 1945 von den Schwierigkeiten der Eisrevue hörte, zögerte er nicht, sondern investierte und erwarb die Stimmenmehrheit. Fast 30 Jahre lang blieb er dem Unternehmen als Geschäftsführer treu. 1973 dann übergab Chalfen die Verantwortung an Skee Goodhart. Doch der Reihe nach:

Bereits 1947 hatte sich HOLIDAY ON ICE fest in den USA etabliert. Die nächsten Tourneen führten das Ensemble deshalb auch in die Ferne: Mexiko, Kuba, Zentral- und Südamerika standen auf dem Programm. 1950 reiste Chalfen voller Ehrgeiz nach Europa – mit dabei hatte er die Top-Stars seiner US-Produktion.

show a week of ticket sales. The show simply wasn't profitable without additional compressors and tanks which would enable the show to change venues without having to wait for the rink to be installed. To turn that idea into a reality would require money, lots of money. The money eventually came from Morris D. Chalfen.

Chalfen was a wealthy businessman and he was absolutely obsessed with figure skating. In 1945 when he heard of the difficulties that the ice skating revue was having he didn't hesitate, he invested and won over the majority of investor votes to become the show's manager. Chalfen was to be the faithful manager of the company for almost 30 years. In 1973 he gave that responsibility to Skee Goodhart.

Looking back HOLIDAY ON ICE had firmly established itself in the USA by 1947. The ensemble then began touring farther afield entertaining audiences in Mexico, Cuba, Central and South America. In 1950 Chalfen ambitiously set off for Europe with the top stars of his US production. The beginning however was anything but encoura-

1993-2003

Seinen 50. Geburtstag feiert HOLIDAY ON ICE in Nizza (Frankreich): Ehemalige und aktive Läufer bilden die längste Kickline der Welt– 1000 Tänzer bewegen sich synchron in einer Reihe. 1999 wird HOLIDAY ON ICE Teil der Stage Holding.

HOLIDAY ON ICE celebrates its 50th Birthday in Nice (France). Active and former skaters form the longest kickline in the world as 1,000 dancers move in one synchronized line. In 1999 HOLIDAY ON ICE becomes part of Stage Holding.

2003/2004

Guinnessbuchrekord: 300 Millionen Zuschauer weltweit haben HOLIDAY ON ICE bisher erlebt. Am 2. Oktober 2003 feiert *Diamonds* in Hamburg Weltpremiere. In seiner 60. Saison, der *Diamond Tour*, präsentiert HOLIDAY ON ICE gleich zwei Shows: *Diamonds* und *Hollywood*.

Another Guiness Book entry, by now 300 million visitors around the world have experienced HOLIDAY ON ICE. The world première of *Diamonds* takes place on October 2nd, 2003 in Hamburg, Germany. During its 60th anniversary *Diamond Tour* HOLIDAY ON ICE presents even two shows: *Diamonds* and *Hollywood*.

Der Beginn jedoch war alles andere als viel versprechend und alles in allem bestand die erste Europa-Tournee aus einem ständigen Auf und Ab.

Bald aber war HOLIDAY ON ICE in ganz Europa bekannt. Ria Baran und Paul Falk – das erste deutsche Nachkriegstraumpaar auf dem Eis – eroberten die Herzen der Zuschauer. Spielend füllten sie 1952 die neu errichtete Dortmunder Westfalenhalle – die damals größte Halle Europas.

Auch die Zusammenarbeit mit Eislaufstar Sonja Henie wurde ab 1952 immer enger. Geschichte machte ihr HOLIDAY ON ICE-Auftritt im Berliner Sportpalast 1953: Sonja Henie, liebevoll ›Häseken‹ genannt, versank in einem Meer von Veilchen, die die begeisterten Zuschauer aufs Eis geworfen hatten.

Die Geschichte von HOLIDAY ON ICE ist voller amüsanter und anrührender Anekdoten – sie allein könnten ein Buch füllen. Wenigstens eine soll nicht unerwähnt bleiben: Der 200-millionste Besucher der Show durfte sich 1970 sehr glücklich schätzen: Er wurde mit Schokolade aufgewogen und hatte bei stattlichen 192 Pfund einiges zu naschen.

ging, and all in all the first European tour was a roller coaster ride.

But soon HOLIDAY ON ICE would be known throughout Europe. Ria Baran and Paul Falk the first ice skating dream pair of post-war Germany captured audiences' hearts. In 1952 they easily filled the newly built Dortmunder Westfallenhalle, the largest arena in Europe at the time.

Starting in 1952 the collaboration with figure skating star Sonja Henie also took on added importance. Her 1953 HOLIDAY ON ICE performance at the Berliner Sportpalast was legendary, Sonja Henie affectionately known as ›Bunny‹, skated in an ocean of violets thrown upon the ice by her enthusiastic fans.

The history of HOLIDAY ON ICE is full of amusing and touching anecdotes which could fill a book of their own. But one has to be shared here. In 1970 the 200 millionth HOLIDAY ON ICE visitor won his weight in chocolate, the chocalate was piled higher and higher until the 192 pound visitor floated in the air upon the sweet scales of HOLIDAY history.

HOLIDAY ON ICE 1959 in Moskau: Empfang bei Ministerpräsident Chruschtschow

HOLIDAY ON ICE visits Moscow in 1959: Reception at the Prime Minister Chruschtschow

HOLIDAY
ON ICE
1958

Extraventura

Unter der Leitung von Anthony van Laast, einem der gefragtesten Regisseure und Choreografen der heutigen Unterhaltungskunst, präsentiert *Extraventura* in einer einmaligen Inszenierung auf einer spektakulären Bühne die schönsten Elemente aus Theater, Oper, Zirkus, Ballett und Musical.

Under the supervision of Anthony van Laast, one of the most sought after directors/choreographers of today's entertainment industry, *Extraventura* presents a unique staging with spectacular sets and the most beautiful elements of theatre, opera, circus, ballet and musical.

Marilyn Monroe – ihr Name bleibt ebenso unvergessen wie ihr Song »Diamonds are a girl's best friend« aus *Blondinen bevorzugt*.

Marilyn Monroe symbolisiert Weiblichkeit, ewige Verlockung und Tragik in einem, ihr Name ist untrennbar mit den ganz Großen aus Politik und Filmgeschäft verknüpft. Die attraktivsten Männer umschwärmen sie – doch ihr Herz bringt nur einer zum Klopfen.

Marilyn Monroe, her name remains as unforgettable as her song »Diamonds are a girl's best friend« from *Gentlemen Prefer Blondes*. Marilyn Monroe symbolizes femininity, timeless temptation and tragedy in one, her name is forever bound to the icons of politics and film. The most eligible men swoon her but her heart is only there for one of them.

Die Rolle des Indiana Jones war Harrison Ford wie auf den Leib geschrieben – und wer kennt ihn nicht, den Abenteuer-Film *Jäger des verlorenen Schatzes?*

HOLIDAY ON ICE lässt die besten Szenen wieder auferstehen: Der waghalsige Forscher und seine Gefährtin werden von Eingeborenen gefangen genommen, als sie mit dem wertvollen heiligen Opferstein zu fliehen versuchen. Die Lage scheint hoffnungslos – gibt es dennoch eine Rettung?

The role of Indiana Jones was tailor-made for Harrison Ford, and who doesn't know the film *Raiders of the Lost Ark*? HOLIDAY ON ICE resurrects the best scenes; the adventurous archaeologist and his accomplice are captured by natives as they try to steal away with priceless sacrificial stones. The situation seems hopeless ... can they be saved?

Weg vom Film, hin zur Musik: Die Beatles prägten mit ihrer Musik, ihren Visionen und ihrem Auftreten mehr als nur eine Generation. Dafür zollt *Extraventura* den vier Pilzköpfen aus Liverpool Tribut und widmet ihnen die Szene »Beatlemania«. In dieser Episode werden die surrealen Fantasien von John Lennon & Co. zu neuem Leben erweckt.

From film to music. With their music, their vision and their performances the Beatles left their mark on more than a generation. Therefore *Extraventura* pays tribute to the four lads from Liverpool with the scene »Beatlemania«, where the surreal fantasies of John Lennon & Co. take on new life.

Auch eine Reminiszenz an die Welt der Oper darf nicht fehlen: Inspiriert von der Musik Giacomo Puccinis wird in der Szene »Butterfly« die tiefe, doch unmögliche Liebe zweier Menschen thematisiert. Inmitten orientalischer Farben und Klänge müssen die beiden erkennen, dass sie zu verschieden sind, um gemeinsam glücklich zu sein.

We cannot forget the world of opera either. Inspired by the music of Giacomo Puccini the scene »Butterfly« presents the deep yet impossible love between two people. In a world of oriental colours and sounds the two lovers must realize that they are too different to ever be happy together.

Die Show endet mit dem Finale, der »Sinfonie auf dem Eis«, bei der mitreißende Musik, rasante Choreografie und ein hohes Maß an sportlichem Können den Zuschauern ein furioses Ende der Show bereiten.

The show ends with »Symphony on Ice« showcasing rousing music, racing choreography and a large dose of athletic ability, giving the audience a furious finale.

Stars

Die großen Stars bei HOLIDAY ON ICE waren nicht allein deshalb so beliebt, weil sie perfekte Dreifach-Sprünge beherrschten. Sie besaßen Show-Talent und konnten auf dem Eis ebenso gut tanzen wie Fred Astaire und Ginger Rogers auf dem Parkett. Viele von ihnen werden unvergessen bleiben. Einige sind wahre Legenden geworden, wie die dreifache Olympiasiegerin, zehnfache Weltmeisterin und sechsfache Europameisterin Sonja Henie: Ihre Sambas, Rumbas und Calypsos sorgten für Furore, von ihren Fans wurde sie liebevoll ›Häseken‹ genannt.

Auch Paare wie die atemberaubende Marika Kilius und der Frauenschwarm Hans-Jürgen Bäumler, sind unsterblich geworden. Mit ihrer unvergleichlichen Eleganz schrieben sie deutsche Eiskunstlaufgeschichte. Die ganz Großen seien hier vorgestellt.

The great stars of HOLIDAY ON ICE weren't only loved because of their technical skills, they possessed show talent and danced across the ice the way Fred Astaire and Ginger Rogers danced across the parquet. Many of them have become unforgettable and some have become true legends, like the three time Olympic, ten time world and six time European champion Sonja Henie. Affectionately called ›Bunny‹ by her fans, her sambas, rumbas and calypsos caused a sensation wherever she went.

And pairs like the breathtaking Marika Kilius and the dreamy Hans-Jürgen Bäumler, who wrote German figure skating history with their incomparable elegance, have become immortal. Here is a survey of the biggest stars of HOLIDAY ON ICE.

Dick Button (USA)

Olympiasieger 1948 und 1952
Weltmeister 1948-1952

Er ist einer der größten Eiskunstläufer aller Zeiten. Während seiner Amateurlaufbahn gelang Dick Button als Erstem und bisher Einzigem ein ›Grand Slam‹ des Eiskunstlaufs: Gold bei den US-Amerikanischen Meisterschaften, den Nord-Amerika-, Europa- und Weltmeisterschaften sowie bei den Olympischen Spielen – und das alles in einem Jahr.

Olympic champion 1948, 1952
World champion 1948-1952

Dick Button was one of the all time greats of figure skating. As an amateur he was the first and to this day only person to ever win the ›Grand Slam‹ of figure skating: In one year he won gold at the US championships, the North American championships, the European championships, the world championships and the Olympics.

Ria Baran & Paul Falk (D)

Olympiasieger 1952
Weltmeister 1951 und 1952
Europameister 1951 und 1952

Das Engagement des Traumpaares Ria Baran und Paul Falk bei HOLIDAY ON ICE sorgte für große Aufregung – waren sie doch die ersten deutschen Stars der Revue. So gelang es den beiden während ihres ersten Gastspiels mit Leichtigkeit, die Dortmunder Westfalenhalle – damals mit 12.000 Plätzen die größte Halle Europas – 29mal bis auf den letzten Platz zu füllen.

Olympic champions 1952
World champions 1951, 1952
European champions 1951, 1952

The signing of the dream pair Ria Baran and Paul Falk at HOLIDAY ON ICE caused unbridled excitement as they were the first German stars to join the show. They sold out their first engagement at the 12,000 seat Dortmunder Westfallenhalle, the largest arena in Europe at the time, for all 29 shows.

Sonja Henie (N)

Olympiasiegerin 1928, 1932,1936
Weltmeisterin 1927-1936
Europameisterin 1931-1936

Zweifelsohne ist sie der größte Eislaufstar aller Zeiten und war ihrer Zeit sportlich um Längen voraus.

Kaum hatte sie ihre Amateurlaufbahn beendet, eroberte Sonja Henie Hollywood für sich. Mehr als zehn Jahre lang sorgte sie regelmäßig für Kassenschlager von 20th Century Fox. Ihre Filme lösten eine regelrechte Eislauf-Hysterie aus. Besonders brillierte die Norwegerin mit ihren Sambas, Rumbas, Calypsos und Hula-Tänzen.

Sonja Henie war vom Eiskunstlauf besessen (selbst mit drei gebrochenen Rippen lief sie ihre Show) und konnte auf eine riesige Fangemeinde zählen. HOLIDAY ON ICE blieb sie auch nach ihrem letzten Engagement, der Südamerika-Tournee 1956, ihr Leben lang treu.
Das letzte öffentliche Foto von Sonja Henie entstand am 5. Oktober 1969 auf der HOLIDAY ON ICE-Premiere in Lausanne, eine Woche vor ihrem Tod. Sie starb am 12. Oktober 1969 im Alter von nur 57 Jahren an Leukämie.

Olympic champion 1928, 1932, 1936
World champion 1927-1936
European champion 1931-1936

Sonja Henie is undoubtedly the greatest ice skating star of all time and she was years ahead of her time athletically.

Sonja Henie had barely finished her amateur career when she conquered Hollywood. For more than ten years she produced blockbusters on a regular basis for 20th Century Fox. The Norwegian sparkled with her sambas, rumbas, calypsos and hula dance numbers.

Sonja Henie lived for ice skating (she was even known to have performed with three broken ribs) and she had an enormous fan base. She remained true to HOLIDAY ON ICE her whole life long, from her last performance on the South American tour of 1956 to her last public photo at the Luzern première on October 5, 1969, one week before her death. Sonja Henie died of leukaemia on October 12th, 1969, she was 57 years old.

Alain Giletti (F)

Weltmeister 1960
Europameister 1955-1957, 1960, 1961

Ab 1962 lief der fünffache Europameister bei verschiedenen Produktionen wie *Indian* für HOLIDAY ON ICE.

World champion 1960
European champion 1955-1957, 1960, 1961

After 1962 the five-time European champion skated in several HOLIDAY ON ICE productions such as *Indian*.

Hayes Alan Jenkins (USA)

Olympiasieger 1956
Weltmeister 1953-1956

Der Amerikaner wechselte direkt im Anschluss an seine Amateurlaufbahn zu HOLIDAY ON ICE.

Olympic champion 1956
World champion 1953-1956

The American came directly to HOLIDAY ON ICE after ending his amateur career.

Silvia & Michel Grandjean (CH)

Europameister 1954

Das elegante Paar wusste besonders mit den Gastspielen *Nussknacker* und *Musik aus Amerika* zu begeistern.

European champions 1954

The elegant couple knew how to thrill crowds especially with their *Nutcracker* and *Music from America* numbers.

Hannerl Walter (A)

Europameisterin 1959

Nach ihrem Titelgewinn war sie Stargast in der HOLIDAY ON ICE-Show *Der Zauberer von Oz.*

European champion 1959

After winning her title Hannerl Walter became a guest star in the HOLIDAY ON ICE show *The Wizard of Oz.*

Hanna Eigel (A)

Europameisterin 1955 und 1957

Von der Wiener Eisrevue zu HOLIDAY ON ICE: Mit großer Leichtigkeit und Grazie zog Hanna Eigel das Publikum in ihren Bann.

European champion 1955, 1957

From the Vienna Ice Revue to HOLIDAY ON ICE, Hanna Eigel mesmerized audiences with her lightness and grace.

Petra Burka (CAN)

Weltmeisterin 1965

In den Niederlanden geboren und in Kanada aufgewachsen, wurde sie von ihrer Mutter – einer ehemaligen Eiskunstläuferin und Niederländischen Meisterin – trainiert.

World champion 1965

Born in the Netherlands and raised in Canada, she was trained by her mother who was a former Dutch Championship winning figure skater.

Diane Towler & Bernard Ford (GB)

Weltmeister 1966-1969
Europameister 1966-1969
Britische Meister 1965-1968

Das attraktive Paar war in Europa und Amerika gleichermaßen beliebt.

World champions 1966-1969
European champions 1966-1969
British champions 1965-1968

The attractive couple was loved in Europe as well as in America.

Emmerich Danzer (A)

Weltmeister 1966-1968

Der talentierte Emmerich Danzer zeigte bei der Olympiade 1968 die wohl beste und waghalsigste Kür von allen – und ging dennoch leer aus. Seiner Beliebtheit beim Publikum tat dies keinen Abbruch.

World champion 1966-1968

The talented Emmerich Danzer performed arguably the best and most daring programme at the 1968 Olympics, yet he went home empty-handed. However, this had no adverse effect on his extreme popularity.

Sjoukje Dijkstra (NL)

Olympiasiegerin 1964
Weltmeisterin 1962-1964
Europameisterin 1960-1962 und 1964

Zwischen 1967 und 1971 begeisterte Sjoukje Dijkstra bei drei HOLIDAY ON ICE-Produktionen ihre Fans in ganz Europa. In dieser Zeit entstand eine tiefe Freundschaft zwischen Sjoukje und dem deutschen Eiskunstlauf-Paar Margret Göbl und Franz Ningel.

Olympic champion 1964
World champion 1962-1964
European champion 1960-1962 and 1964

Sjoukje Dijkstra thrilled her fans throughout Europe in three HOLIDAY ON ICE productions between 1967 and 1971. It was also during this time that a deep friendship developed between Sjoukje and the German skating pair of Margret Göbl and Franz Ningel.

Donald McPherson (Can)

Weltmeister 1963

Schon während seiner Amateurlaufbahn weltberühmt, entwickelte er sich im Profilager zu einer der größten Persönlichkeiten des Eiskunstsports. Er gehörte mit seinem furiosen Stil zur ersten Garde der Eiskunstläufer.

World champion 1963

World famous during his amateur career, McPherson developed into one of the great personalities of professional figure skating. His furious style placed him in the upper ranks of figure skating history.

Eva & Pavel Roman (CSSR)

Weltmeister 1962-1965
Europameister 1964 und 1965

Die Geschwister dominierten in ihrer Amateurlaufbahn für viele Jahre die Szene und haben Eiskunstlauf-Geschichte geschrieben.

World champions 1962-1965
European champions 1964 and 1965

The brother/sister duo dominated the scene for several years during their amateur career and wrote figure skating history along the way.

Hana Maskova (CSSR)

Europameisterin 1968

Hana Maskova hatte eine riesige Fangemeinde – bis sie durch einen schrecklichen Autounfall mitten aus dem Leben gerissen wurde.

European champion 1968

Hana Maskova had an enormous fan following up until the time she was killed in a tragic automobile accident.

Joan Haanappel (NL)

Holländische Meisterin 1956-1958 und 1960

Die Holländerin hatte eine tiefgründige Ausstrahlung. Sie erreichte ein perfektes Zusammenspiel von eisläuferischer Perfektion, künstlerischem Einfühlungsvermögen und Ausdruckskraft.

Dutch champion 1956-1958 and 1960

Joan Haanappel had charisma through and through. She achieved a perfect balance between ice skating perfection, artistic sensibility and expression.

Margret Göbl & Franz Ningel (D)

Deutsche Meister 1960-1962

Margret Göbl und Franz Ningel – während ihrer Amateurlaufbahn die Erzrivalen von Marika Kilius und Hans-Jürgen Bäumler – waren besonders schnelle und rhythmische Läufer.

German champions 1960-1962

The exceptionally fast and rhythmic skating pair of Margret Göbl and Franz Ningel were the arch rivals of Marika Kilius and Hans-Jürgen Bäumler during their amateur careers.

Alexej N. Ulanov (UDSSR)

Olympiasieger 1972
Weltmeister 1969-1972
Europameister 1969-1972

Alexej Ulanov war während seiner Amateurlaufbahn besonders durch seine Paarläufe mit Irina Rodnina berühmt. Hier ist er mit Ljudmila Smirnova zu sehen.

Olympic champion 1972
World champion 1969-1972
European champion 1969-1972

During his amateur career Alexej Ulanov became especially popular through his pairs performances with Irina Rodnina. He is pictured here with Ljudmila Smirnova.

Ondrej Nepela (CSSR)

Olympiasieger 1972
Weltmeister 1971-1973
Europameister 1969-1973

Nachdem er seine dritte Weltmeisterschaft gewonnen hatte, unterschrieb Ondrej Nepala 1973 in seiner Heimatstadt Bratislava den Vertrag mit HOLIDAY ON ICE. Besonders berühmt wurde er durch seine Grazie und die Eleganz seiner Bewegungen.

Olympic champion 1972
World champion 1971-1973
European champion 1969-1973

In 1973 after winning his third world championship Ondrej Nepela signed a contract with HOLIDAY ON ICE in his home town of Bratislava. He became especially famous for the grace and elegance of his movements.

Trixi Schuba (A)

Olympiasiegerin 1972
Weltmeisterin 1971 und 1972
Europameisterin 1972

Die Österreicherin unterschrieb 1974 ihren Vertrag bei HOLIDAY ON ICE und glänzte in der Show *25th Anniversary.*

Olympic champion 1972
World champion 1971 and 1972
European champion 1972

The Austrian signed on with HOLIDAY ON ICE in 1974 and shined in the *25th Anniversary* show.

Toller Cranston (CAN)

Kanadischer Meister 1971-1976

Seine ganz besondere Ausdruckskraft prägte eine ganze Generation von Eiskunstläufern. Toller Cranston war exzentrisch und skurril – er verkörperte die Avantgarde des Eiskunstlaufs.

Canadian champion 1971-1976

His special expressive power influenced an entire generation of skaters. Toller Cranston was excentric and odd, he was the embodiment of the avant-garde in figure skating.

Claudia Kristofics-Binder (A)

Europameisterin 1982

Ihre Musikalität, Eleganz und künstlerische Ausdruckskraft waren lange unübertroffen.

European champion 1982

Her musicality, elegance and artistic expression were incomparable for years.

Gudrun Hauss & Walter Häfner (D)

Deutsche Meister 1969

Fast 20 Jahre lang hielt dieses elegante Paar HOLIDAY ON ICE die Treue.

German champions 1969

This elegant couple stayed faithful to HOLIDAY ON ICE for nearly 20 years.

Marika Kilius & Hans-Jürgen Bäumler (D)

Weltmeister 1963 und 1964
Europameister 1959-1964
Deutsche Meister 1958, 1959, 1963 und 1964

Ihr Erfolg und ihre Ausstrahlung machten die Doppelweltmeister und sechsfachen Europameister zum Traumpaar. Die Medien folgten Marika Kilius und Hans-Jürgen Bäumler auf Schritt und Tritt. In Deutschland waren beide populärer als Filmstars. Unmittelbar nach der Weltmeisterschaft 1964 gelang es HOLIDAY, das Paar für eine bis dahin noch nie da gewesene Gage zu verpflichten. Bei HOLIDAY ON ICE begeisterten die beiden mit der *Gypsy Dolly* Show und sorgten für Zuschauerrekorde. Die Deutschland-Tournee war bis auf den letzten Platz ausverkauft.
Das Traumpaar lief noch bis 1981 in verschiedenen Inszenierungen von HOLIDAY ON ICE.

World chamions 1963 and 1964
European champions 1959-1964
German champions 1958, 1959, 1963 and 1964

Their success and charisma made the two-time world and six-time European champions a dream pair. The media followed Marika Kilius and Hans-Jürgen Bäumler wherever they went. In Germany the two were more popular than movie stars. Shortly after their world championship victory they secured contracts with HOLIDAY ON ICE for salaries that were unheard of at the time. There the two thrilled fans with their *Gypsy Dolly* show and set attendance records wherever they performed. Their German tours were consistantly sold out.
The dream pair skated in various HOLIDAY ON ICE productions until 1981.

Denise Biellmann (CH)

Weltmeisterin 1981
Europameisterin 1981

Weltbekannt wurde die Schweizerin durch ihre waghalsige Biellmann-Pirouette. Mit immer neuen, eigenwilligen und modernen Kür-Kreationen sorgte sie während ihrer Amateurlaufbahn für Begeisterungsstürme – und verzauberte auch die Zuschauer von HOLIDAY ON ICE.

World champion 1981
European champion 1981

The Swiss star became world famous with her daring Biellmann Pirouette. During her amateur career and later with HOLIDAY ON ICE she thrilled and mesmerized crowds with unique, new and modern programme creations.

Rudi Cerne (D)

Vize-Europameister 1984
Deutscher Meister 1978 und 1980

HOLIDAY ON ICE nahm den sympathischen Läufer aus Herne direkt nach dessen Amateurlaufbahn unter Vertrag. Drei Jahre lang blieb Rudi Cerne der Show treu und reiste mit ihr durch ganz Europa.

European championship silver medalist 1984
German champion 1978 and 1980

HOLIDAY ON ICE signed the likeable skater from Herne immediately after the end of his amateur career. Rudi Cerne was faithful to the show for three years and toured throughout Europe.

Claudia Leistner (D)

Europameisterin 1989
Deutsche Meisterin 1985-1989

Trotz vieler Verletzungen gab sie nie auf. In ihren zwei Jahren bei HOLIDAY ON ICE konnte Claudia Leistner das tun, was sie am liebsten mochte: das Publikum begeistern.

European champion 1989
German champion 1985-1989

She never gave up despite her many injuries. In the two years that she was with HOLIDAY ON ICE Claudia Leistner was able to do what she loved most, thrill crowds.

Norbert Schramm (D)

Deutscher Meister 1979, 1981 und 1984
Europameister 1982, 1983

Der deutsche Eisprinz unterschrieb 1986 seinen Vertrag – und blieb der Truppe sieben Jahre lang erhalten. Mit seiner Leidenschaft, seinen eigenen Kreationen und speziellen Effekten wie den Rückwärtssalti faszinierte Norbert Schramm das Publikum.

German champion 1979, 1981 and 1984
European champion 1982 and 1983

The German 'Ice Prince' signed on with HOLIDAY ON ICE in 1986 and stayed with the show for seven years. Norbert Schramm fascinated crowds with his passion, his individual creations and special effects such as his famous back flips.

Robin Cousins (GB)

Olympiasieger 1980
Europameister 1980

Robin Cousins konnte im Laufe seiner Karriere immer wieder neue Maßstäbe setzen: Nach seinem Gold bei den Olympischen Spielen errang er drei Profi-Weltmeistertitel im Eiskunstlauf. Später spielte er Hauptrollen in Musicals, trat als Solist bei HOLIDAY ON ICE auf und choreografierte zahlreiche Eis- und Tanzshows.

Mehrere HOLIDAY ON ICE-Produktionen wie *Celebration* und *Hollywood* tragen seine Handschrift als Choreograf bzw. Regisseur

Olympic champion 1980
European champion 1980

Over the course of his career Robin Cousins set new levels of excellence. After winning Olympic gold he won three world professional championship titles. Later he went on to play leading roles in musicals, became a soloist for HOLIDAY ON ICE and did the choreographies of several skating and dance shows. Many HOLIDAY ON ICE productions such as *Celebration* and *Hollywood* bore his signature as choreographer and director.

Marina Kielmann (D)

Vize-Europameisterin 1992
Deutsche Meisterin 1990-1993

Marina Kielmann kennzeichnet ein gestenreicher Laufstil, der Sportlichkeit, Eleganz und künstlerische Ausdrucksfähigkeit vereint. Die Dortmunderin war die erste Eissport-Amateurin, die mit Erlaubnis der Deutschen Eislauf-Union (DEU) professionell auftreten durfte.

European championship
German champion 1990-1993

Marina Kielmann embodied a gestural style which combined athletic prowess, elegance and artistic expression. The skater from Dortmund was the first amateur to be allowed to perform professionally by the German Ice Skating Union (DEU).

Katarina Witt (DDR/D)

Olympiasiegerin 1984 und 1988
Weltmeisterin 1984, 1985, 1987 und 1988
Europameisterin 1983-1988
Achtfache Nationale Meisterin

Die erfolgreichste Läuferin nach Sonja Henie begann ihre Karriere in der früheren DDR. Bereits 1988 – noch vor dem Fall der Mauer zwischen dem Ost- und dem Westteil Deutschlands – kam Katarina Witt zu HOLIDAY ON ICE. Der Revue war damals mit ihrer Verpflichtung also ein großes Kunststück gelungen.

Während ihrer Amateurlaufbahn war sie die Künstlerin, die ihren Auftritten den einheitlichsten Stil gab: Musik, Kostüm, Make-up und Choreografie – alles war perfekt aufeinander abgestimmt. 1983 sorgte sie als junger Mozart in Hosen statt des obligatorischen Eislaufrocks für Aufruhr.

Nachdem Katarina Witt 1988 sowohl Europa- als auch Weltmeisterin und zum zweiten Mal Olympiasiegerin geworden war, wechselte sie vom Amateur- ins Profilager der Eiskunstläufer. Ihr Debüt bei HOLIDAY ON ICE gab die Ausnahmeläuferin in der Show *In 80 Tagen um die Welt.* Dabei sorgte sie 1988 und 1989 von Zürich bis Stockholm für Zuschauerrekorde.

Später nutzte Katarina Witt HOLIDAY ON ICE als perfekte Vorbereitung auf ihr Comeback 1994 bei den Olympischen Spielen in Lillehammer. Auch diese Showsaison brachte ihr die uneingeschränkte Zuneigung des – dieses Mal englischen – Publikums.

Olympic champion 1984 and 1988
World champion 1984, 1985, 1987 and 1988
European champion 1983-1988
Eight-time national champion

The most successful women's figure skater since Sonja Henie, started her career in East Germany. Katarina Witt joined HOLIDAY ON ICE in 1988 before the fall of the Berlin Wall. The fact that HOLIDAY managed to sign her bordered on the miraculous.

During her amateur career she created a new level of all around style, in which music, costume, make-up and choreography were perfectly meshed. She caused a sensation in 1983 by performing as a young Wolgang Amadeus Mozart wearing trousers instead of the obligatory figure skating skirt.

In 1988 after becoming European as well as World champion and winning her second Olympic gold, she turned professional. Her HOLIDAY ON ICE debut came in the show *Around the World in 80 Days*, a show in which the star drew record audiences from Zurich to Stockholm in 1988 and 1989.

Later Katarina Witt used HOLIDAY ON ICE as the perfect preparation for her 1994 Olympic comeback in Lillehammer. This show season would bring her the praise of her, this time, English audience.

Isabelle & Paul Duchesnay (F)

Weltmeister 1991

Das Geschwisterpaar galt als das ›couple terrible‹ des Eiskunstlaufs: frech, wild und modern.

World champions 1991

The brother and sister duo was considered the ›couple terrible‹ of ice skating, cheeky, wild and modern.

Philippe Candeloro (F)

Französischer Meister 1993-1996

Der attraktive Franzose gilt mit Fug und Recht als Superstar auf dem Eis. Seine riesige – vor allem weibliche – Fangemeinde lässt daran keinen Zweifel aufkommen.

French champion 1993-1996

The handsome Frenchman took to the ice with the style and confidence of a superstar. His huge following of mostly female fans erased any claims to the contrary.

Surya Bonaly (F)

Europameisterin 1991-1994
Französische Meisterin 1988-1993

Als eine der ganz großen Eiskunstläuferinnen verblüffte sie immer wieder durch ihre Akrobatik. So war sie die einzige Frau, die einen Rückwärtssalto sauber in ihre Darbietung einbaute.

European champion 1991-1994
French champion 1988-1993

One of the greats of figure skating, she astounded crowds again and again with her acrobatics. She was the only woman to include a back flip in her programme.

Radka Kovarikova & René Novotny (Tschechien)

Weltmeister 1995
Europameister 1996

Sie waren das erste tschechische Paar, das sich eine Goldmedaille bei Weltmeisterschaften holte. Nach dem Titelgewinn heirateten sie und wechselten anschließend ins Profilager.

World champions 1995
European champions 1996

They were the first couple from the Czech Republic to win gold at the world championships. After winning the title they married and turned professional.

Andrej Vlachtchenko (D)

Lettischer Meister 1992 und 1993
Deutscher Meister 1995 und 1996

Andrej Vlachtchenko sprang den gefürchteten dreifachen Axel bei internationalen Wettkämpfen.

Latvian champion 1992 and 1993
German champion 1995 and 1996

Andrej Vlachtchenko regularly performed the feared triple axel in international competition.

Mandy Wötzel & Ingo Steuer (D)

Deutsche Meister 1992, 1993, 1995-1997
Europameister 1995
Weltmeister 1997

Das deutsche Weltklasse-Paar raubt mit seinen extravaganten Hebungen und seinem waghalsigen Stil ganzen Hallen den Atem. Das HOLIDAY ON ICE-Publikum erlebt zwei Stars, die sich elegant in die Inszenierungen einpassen. Zugleich präsentieren beide ihre eigenen Choreografien mit großer Professionalität und viel Liebe zum Detail.

German champions 1992, 1993, 1995-1997
European champions 1995
World champions 1997

The world class German duo took away audience's breath with extravagant lifts and daring style. HOLIDAY ON ICE audience witnessed two stars who skated elegantly into a set scene, as well as a couple who presented their own choreography with professionalism and attention to detail.

Marina Anissina & Gwendal Peizerat (F)

Olympiasieger 2002
Weltmeister 2000
Europameister 2000 und 2002
Französische Meister 1996-2001

Sie gehören zweifelsohne zur Weltspitze der Eistänzer. Ihre Technik ist brillant – besonders bestechend ist jedoch ihre künstlerische Ausdrucksfähigkeit.

Olympic champions 2002
World champions 2000
European champions 2000 and 2002
French champions 1996-2001

Without a doubt one of the best ice dancing couples in the world. Their technique is brilliant and their artistic expression is especially captivating.

In Concert

Die erste HOLIDAY ON ICE-Inszenierung des dritten Jahrtausends setzt neue Akzente und bricht mit der Konvention, dass Eiskunstläufer zur Musik vom Band ihr Können unter Beweis stellen. Dabei greift *In Concert* die Tradition der frühen Revuen des letzten Jahrhunderts auf und zeigt zugleich richtungsweisend eine neue Form der Unterhaltung: eine echte Multimediashow mit Projektionen, Lichteffekten, Videoscreens, Livemusik auf verschiedenen Bühnen mit ferngesteuerten Bühnenelementen – und natürlich mit den besten Eiskunstläufern, die die Welt zu bieten hat.

The first HOLIDAY ON ICE staging of the third millenium sets new accents and breaks with the old convention that figure skaters need a band in order to show their skill. At the same time *In Concert* takes up the tradition of the early revues of last century and shows new directions in entertainment: a real multimedia show with projections, lighting effects, video screens, live music on several stages with remote control set elements – and of course the best figure skaters in the world.

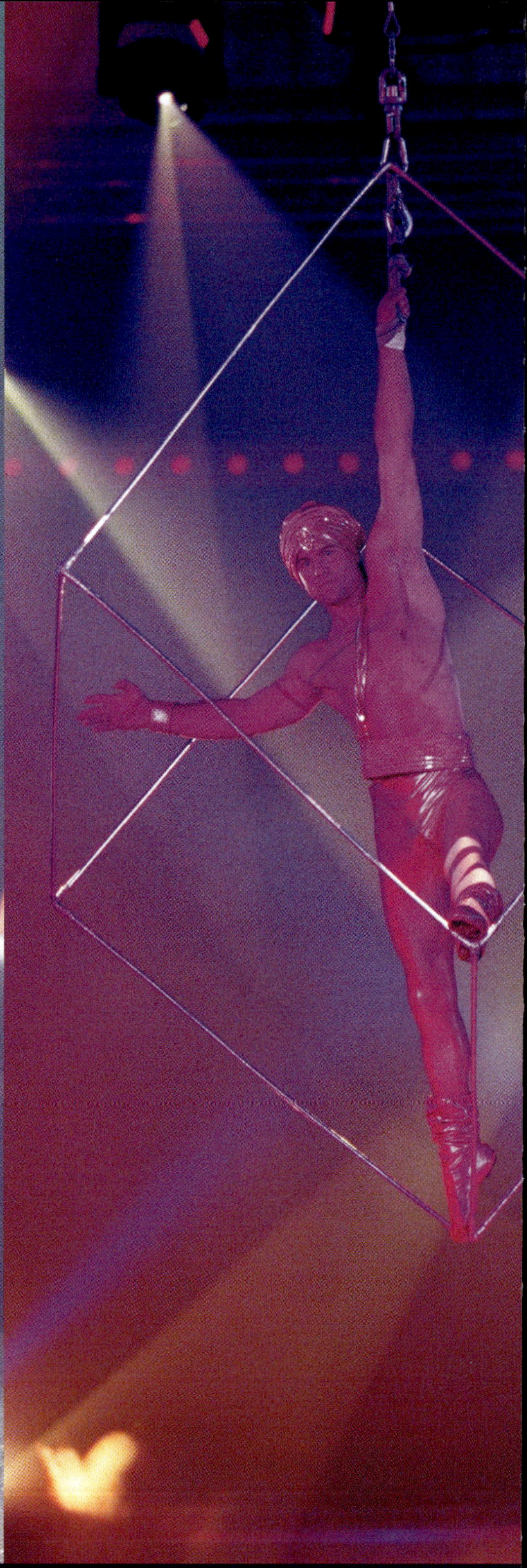

Urbanes Flair und prickelnde Leidenschaft kommen mit Moby auf. Sein Song »Body Rock« ist der Beginn einer energiegeladenen Performance, bei der kurze Szenen gestaltet werden, die parallel auf einem riesigen Videoscreen zu sehen sind. Das letzte Stück der Szene stammt von Enigma – damit beendet das gesamte Ensemble spektakulär die erste Showhälfte.

Urban flair and effervesent passion arise with Moby. His song »Body Rock« kicks off an energized performance where short scenes are constructed and are seen in real time on gigantic video screens. The last piece in the scene is from Enigma, when the entire ensemble brings the first half of the show to a spectacular close.

In Concert präsentiert nicht nur moderne Popmusik – auch die vitale Energie des Folk kommt nicht zu kurz. Mit der Musik von Rodrigo und den Gipsy Kings wird es zuerst spanisch-temperamentvoll. »Driving Old Grey« entführt dann in den Süden der Vereinigten Staaten, genauer gesagt ins lebensbejahende New Orleans. Die Szene endet schließlich mit dem berühmten Violinisten Ludwig Girdland. Die Vitalität des beschwingten irischen Tanzeslieds »The Gravel Walk Jig« ergreift auch die Zuhörer.

In Concert not only showcases modern pop music, the vitality of folk music also features prominently. The show starts with the Spanish temperament of Rodrigo and the Gipsy Kings. With »Driving Old Grey« the journey continues into the old south of the United States, more specifically to the lively city of New Orleans. The scene closes with the famous violinist Ludwig Girdland, where the vitality of the swinging Irish dance tune »The Gravel Walk Jig« captivates the listener.

Bei einer Show wie *In Concert* darf Jazz auf keinen Fall fehlen. Packend und leidenschaftlich interpretiert zuerst der Sololäufer Richard Swenning die Miles Davis-Nummer »L'Ascenseur pour l'echafaud« (Fahrstuhl zum Schaffott), ein faszinierendes Duett für Trompete und Saxophon. Mit dem Wechselspiel von Bewegung und Musik erhält das Stück so eine ganz neue, überaus lebendige Qualität. Im Anschluss beweist dann jeder der Musiker sein Können

You cannot have a show like *In Concert* without jazz. At first the solo skater Richard Swenning gives a gripping and passionate interpretation of Miles Davis' »L'Ascenseur pour l'echafaud« (Lift to the Scaffold), a fascinating duet for trompet and saxophone. The oscillation between movement and music gives the piece a totally new and lively quality. To close every musician flaunts his finesse to the crowd with the pieces »Caravan« and »Birdland«.

Inmitten eines arabischen Altstadtviertels findet sich der Zuschauer bei den wunderschönen und exotischen Klängen von Kevin Nadeaus Komposition »Arabian Nights« wieder.
»Arabian Nights« ist eine elektrisierende Mischung aus der traditionellen Musik des Mittleren Ostens und Elementen westlicher Popmusik: Ein romantisches Märchen nimmt in der Altstadt seinen Lauf. Am Ende der Szene stürmt ein Trupp tanzender Derwische aufs Eis und verbreitet Energie, Leidenschaft und Faszination.

The exotic and wonderful sounds of Kevin Nadeau's »Arabian Nights« move through the air and the audience finds itself in the heart of an old Arabian city. »Arabian Nights« is an electrifying mix of traditional middle eastern music with elements of western pop music – a romantic fairy tale takes place in the alleys of the old city. In the finale a group of whirling dervishes storm onto the ice exuding energy, passion and fascination.

Hinter den Kulissen
Behind the Scenes

»Wie entsteht eigentlich eine Show?« – Diese Frage stellen sich unweigerlich all jene, die von der Perfektion der Produktionen und des Unternehmens HOLIDAY ON ICE beeindruckt sind. Das sind jährlich rund 5 Millionen Besucher weltweit. Wer setzt die Idee, die der Anfang aller Dinge ist, schließlich um?

Jede Show präsentiert bis zu 70 Eisläufer, die in den etwa 1700 Vorstellungen pro Jahr ihr Können unter Beweis stellen.

Woher kommen die vielen Künstler? Wer entwickelt die Choreografie? Wer ist für die Musik verantwortlich, wer für die Kostüme und wer für das Bühnenbild?

Kurzum: Wer hält hinter den Kulissen die Fäden in der Hand, choreografiert, organisiert, entwirft und entwickelt eine Show, die später Millionen von Menschen begeistern wird?

»How does a show actually come about?« Anyone that is impressed by the perfection of a HOLIDAY ON ICE production eventually asks this question. And that means about 5 million people per year, worldwide. Who turns the initial idea into a show?

Each show presents up to 70 skaters, in as many as 1700 performances a year.

Where do all of these performers come from? Who develops the choreography? Who is responsible for the music? Who does the costumes? Who designs the sets?

In short, who pulls the strings behind the scenes? Who choreographs, organizes, plans and develops a show that will play to millions of excited guests?

For example in the current show *Diamonds* more than 50 figure skaters are engaged in a search for

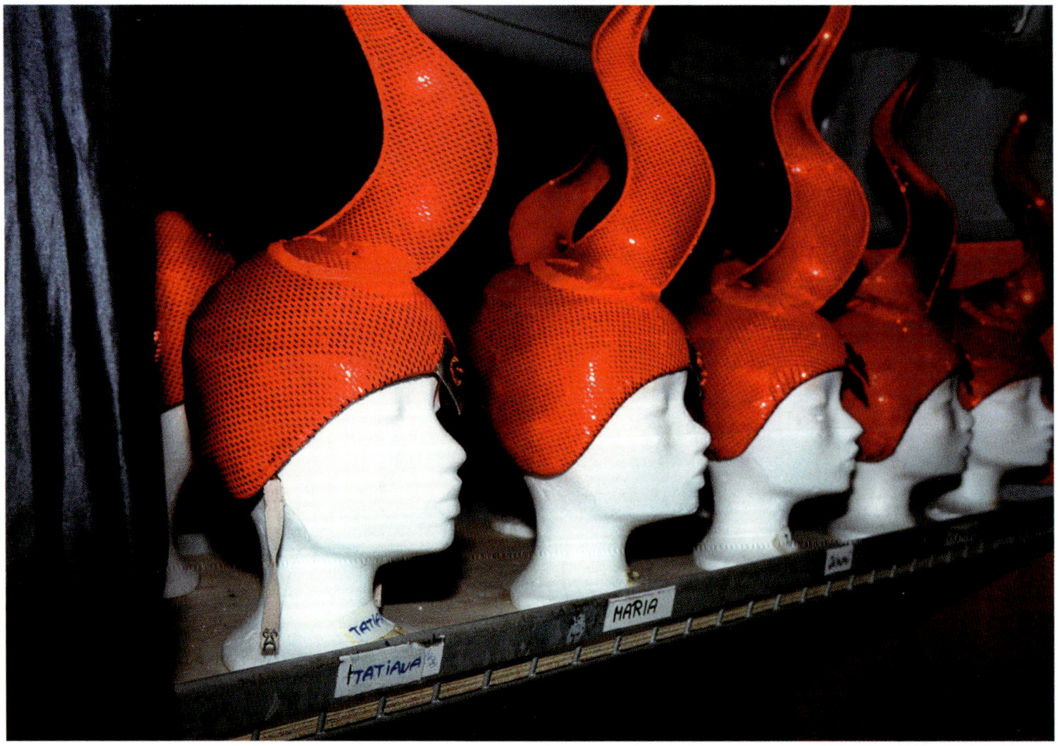

In der aktuellen Show *Diamonds* agieren beispielsweise circa 50 Eiskunstläufer bei der Suche nach dem Stein der Steine. Ihr Weg führt sie durch spannende Abenteuer und romantische Liebeleien: Eben noch bei einem mittelalterlichen Ritterspiel, finden sie sich plötzlich in einem verruchten Nachtclub der 20er Jahre wieder, bis im versunkenen Atlantis das Glück zum Greifen nah ist. Wieder einmal wurden in einer Produktion neue Maßstäbe gesetzt, schließlich lautet das Leitmotiv der 60-jährigen HOLIDAY ON ICE-Geschichte: Niemals sollte man sich auf den gewonnenen Lorbeeren ausruhen, niemals denken, man sei angekommen. Immer wieder aufs Neue werden deshalb die Shows dem neuesten Stand der Licht- und Tontechnik angepasst.

Was für die Technik gilt, trifft ebenso für das künstlerische Ausdrucksvermögen der Eisläufer zu. Figuren, die früher nur Solisten beherrschten, sind mittlerweile Standard für das ganze Ensemble. Die

the ›stone of stones‹. Their journey takes them on a spectacular adventure and romantic escapades. First to a medieval knight's competition, which then suddenly leads to a 1920's nightclub, only to end up in Atlantis where the treasure is in sight. Each show sets new standards of excellence true to the guiding maxim of HOLIDAY ON ICE's 60 year history which dictates ›never rest on your laurels, and never tell yourself that you've made it‹. This is why each show is on the cutting edge of lighting and sound technology, as well as artistic expression.

Moves that formerly belonged to the repertoire of the solo stars are now the standard for the entire ensemble. The soloists perform jumps and lifts that were unimaginable in the past. Naturally music, costume and set design have also changed tremendously over the years. All in all a production costs about 5 million Euro, yet this sum can easily be doubled.

NATASHA

Solisten zeigen heute Sprünge und Hebungen, die vor Jahren unvorstellbar schienen. Natürlich haben sich auch Musik, Kostümdesign und Bühne im Laufe der Jahre enorm verändert. Alles in allem kostet eine Produktion mittlerweile insgesamt ungefähr 5 Millionen Euro – doch kann dieser Betrag auch leicht einmal verdoppelt werden.

Jede Show beginnt mit einer Idee, einem Grundkonzept. Als Inspirationsquelle dafür können eine Filmszene, ein Song oder etwas ganz anderes dienen. Diese Grundidee wird vom Kreativteam, darunter Regisseur und Choreograf, in Szenen umgesetzt.

Robin Cousins, Olympiasieger und mehrfacher Weltmeister im Eiskunstlauf, ist als Co-Regisseur maßgeblich an der Umsetzung des Konzepts der Show *Diamonds* beteiligt. Cousins, der bereits frühere HOLIDAY ON ICE-Produktionen mitentwickelt hat, muss den kreativen Prozess überblicken und dafür sorgen, dass die ursprüngliche Vision auf bestmögliche Weise zum Leben erweckt wird. Der Co-Regisseur wählt gemeinsam mit der Regisseurin und Choreografin die anderen Kreativen und den Cast, also die Eistänzer, aus.

Every show starts with an idea, or a concept. The source of inspiration can be a film scene, a song or something else completely. This concept is then developed further by a creative team, including the director and the choreographer who transform the idea into a scene.

Olympic and world figure skating champion Robin Cousins is responsible to a large degree for the transformation of the show *Diamonds* which he co-directs. Cousins, who has worked on many HOLIDAY ON ICE productions in the past, oversees the creative process and makes sure that the initial vision is brought to life in the best possible way. The co-director chooses the creative team and the ice dancers, together with his director and choreographer.

Two time Emmy winner Sarah Kawahara is the director and choreographer. Kawahara, who has known Cousins for 20 years, was most recently honoured for her choreography of the opening ceremonies of the Winter Olympics in Salt Lake City. In the first phases of the *Diamonds* show the two of them sketched out the entire choreography

Sarah Kawahara, Regisseurin und Choreografin, ist zweifache Emmy-Preisträgerin: Zuletzt wurde sie für ihre Choreografie der Eröffnungszeremonie bei den Olympischen Winterspielen in Salt Lake City geehrt. Sie und Robin Cousins kennen sich schon seit 20 Jahren. In einem der ersten Schritte für die *Diamonds*-Show haben beide die Choreografie auf Papier skizziert. Später mussten die Läufer ihre Schritte mit allergrößter Präzision einstudieren. Für die Proben sind etwa 6 Wochen vorgesehen. Natürlich haben auch die Eiskunstläufer ein Mitspracherecht: Besonders die Solisten sollen sich in ihren Rollen wohl fühlen, denn die Eisläufer sind es schließlich, die die Show jeden Tag aufführen – an Samstagen sogar dreimal. Dabei merkt das Publikum schnell, ob sie mit ganzem Herzen dabei sind.

HOLIDAY ON ICE-Bühnenbildner Marc Fisher arbeitete bereits mit Show-Größen wie Elton John, den Rolling Stones und Tina Turner. Seine Erfahrung in der Gestaltung von Rockbühnen kommt Fisher für die gigantischen Dimensionen von *Diamonds* zugute. Einen seiner Entwürfe musste der Executive Producer Peter O'Keeffe dennoch ablehnen: Das 11 Meter hohe Bühnenbild hätte nicht in allen HOLIDAY ON ICE-Hallen aufgestellt werden können.

on a piece of paper. Later during six weeks of rehearsals the skaters learned to complete the figures with absolute precision. Of course the skaters can also put in their ideas, primarily the soloists need to feel good about what they are doing because in the end it is they who have to carry the show every day (and three times on Saturdays!). The audience can quickly tell if their heart is in it or not.

HOLIDAY ON ICE set designer Marc Fisher has worked with show greats such as Elton John, the Rolling Stones and Tina Turner. His experience in designing rock concert stages helped Fisher tackle the gigantic dimensions of the Diamonds set. Unfortunately not all of his designs could be realized, executive producer Peter O'Keeffe had to veto the construction of one, 11 meter tall set as it could not be installed in all of the venues that HOLIDAY ON ICE would be playing.

Peter O'Keeffe has the difficult task of finding a balance between creative desires and technical possibilities.

What would a show be without music? It is practically inconceivable! The melodies have to trans-

Peter O'Keeffe obliegt die schwere Aufgabe, eine Balance zwischen kreativem Entfaltungswunsch und technischer Realisierbarkeit zu finden.

Was wäre eine Show ohne Musik? Das ist kaum vorstellbar!

Die Melodien sollen das Thema der Show transportieren und die Zuschauer mitreißen.

So ist die Wahl des musikalischen Leiters einer Produktion von großer Bedeutung – für *Diamonds* ist sie auf Emilio Kauderer gefallen. Bekannt für seine Filmmusik zu großen Hollywood-Filmen, komponierte Kauderer Stücke zum Teil exklusiv für *Diamonds*. Darüber hinaus arrangierte er Hits der Gipsy Kings, von Pink Floyd, Michael Jackson, Shakira und Coolio. Die endgültige Auswahl hat Emilio Kauderer gemeinsam mit Regisseurin und Choreografin Sarah Kawahara und Co-Regisseur Robin Cousins getroffen.

Wie vorangegangene HOLIDAY ON ICE-Produktionen auch, präsentiert *Diamonds* etwa 300 der kunstvollsten Kostüme: Kreiert haben sie Modeschöpfer Rudolph Moshammer und Kostümdesigner Frank Krenz.

port the theme of the show and get the audience excited.

That is why the choice of musical director is so important, and for *Diamonds* the choice came down to Emilio Kauderer. Known for his compositions for big Hollywood films and his arrangements on hits by the Gipsy Kings, Pink Floyd, Michael Jackson, Shakira and Coolio, Kauderer composed pieces exclusively for Diamonds. The final musical decisions were made by Emilio Kauderer together with director and choreographer Sarah Kawahara and co-director Robin Cousins.

As with previous HOLIDAY ON ICE productions, *Diamonds* features about 300 artistic costumes, these were all created by fashion designer Rudolph Moshammer and costume designer Frank Krenz.

As is the case with the choreographer, the designer is in constant dialogue with the skaters, because in the end they are the ones who have to wear the costumes. If they don't feel good in their costumes, it has a direct effect on their perfor-

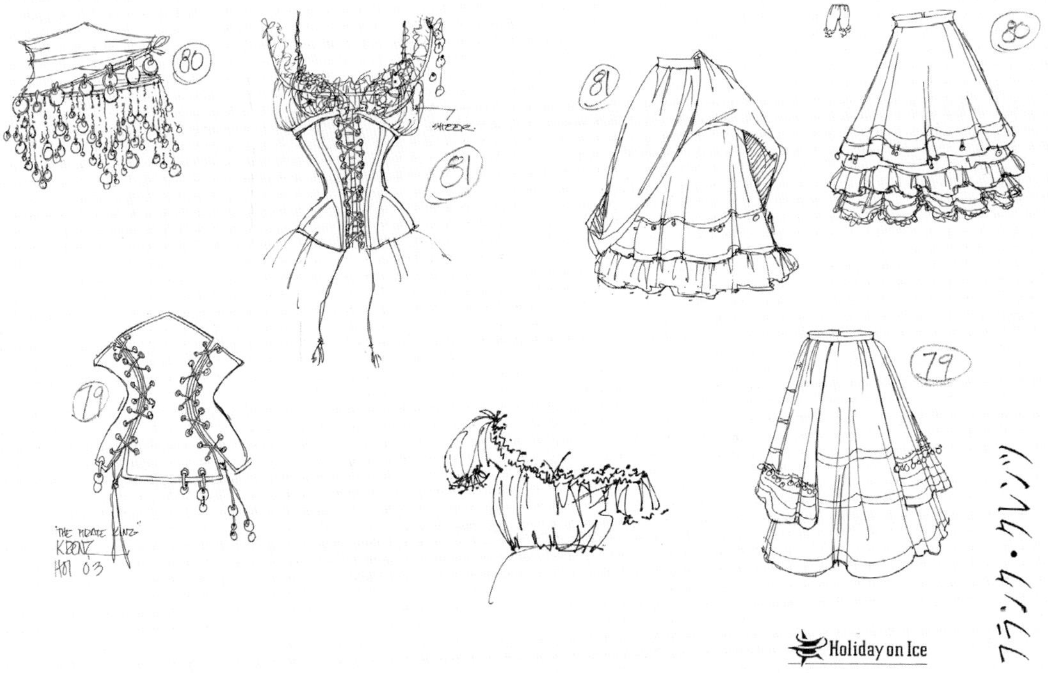

Holiday on Ice

Skizzen von Frank Krenz, der Kostüme für *Diamonds* kreiert hat.

Sketches by Frank Krenz, who has designed costumes for *Diamonds*.

Die Skizzen von Rudolph Moshammer für das Diamanten-Kleid.

Rudolph Moshammer's sketches for the Diamond Dress.

Holiday on Ice
DIAMOND TOUR
Diamonds

Ähnlich wie der Choreograf steht auch der Designer in ständigem Dialog mit den Künstlern auf dem Eis – schließlich sind sie es, die die Kostüme tragen müssen. Wenn sie sich in ihren Kostümen unbehaglich fühlen würden, hätte dies unweigerlich Auswirkung auf die Darbietung. Allerdings sollten die Kostüme trotz aller Änderungswünsche noch miteinander harmonieren. Kompromisse müssen also gefunden werden, mit denen alle Beteiligten zufrieden sind.

Aber was wären die Kreativen und ihre Ideen ohne die Eiskunstläufer? Die Tänzer bilden das Herz der Show, sie verzaubern das Publikum. Ihre Ausstrahlung lässt eine Aufführung unvergesslich werden.

HOLIDAY ON ICE sucht deshalb kontinuierlich nach geeigneten Talenten: Fast wöchentlich finden Vortanztermine in allen größeren Städten Europas statt. Nachwuchs wird außerdem bei Wettkämpfen gesichtet oder von HOLIDAY ON ICE-Läufern empfohlen. Ein Engagement bekommen nur die Besten: Grundvoraussetzung sind technische Perfektion und schauspielerisches Talent. In jeder Produktion tanzen Darsteller aus ungefähr 15 verschiedenen Nationen. Manche bleiben der HOLIDAY ON ICE-Familie fast ein Leben lang treu – eine Bindung, die für sich spricht.

mance. However, in the end all of the costumes have to harmonize with each other no matter what alterations might be desired. Therefore compromises have to be found, if everyone is to remain happy.

But what would all of these creative people be without the skaters themselves? The dancers are the heart of the show, and they are the ones who excite the audience. Their charisma makes a show unforgettable.

That is why HOLIDAY ON ICE is constantly seeking new talents. Skating auditions take place in every large city in Europe nearly every week. Newcomers are also scouted at competitions or recommended by HOLIDAY ON ICE skaters. Only the best are signed on, the requirements are technical perfection and acting talent. Every production features skaters from about 15 nations. Some remain true to the HOLIDAY ON ICE family their whole life long, which is a commitment that speaks for itself.

Der extravagante Modezar Rudolph Moshammer mit seinem Ein und Alles: der Hundedame Daisy.

The extravagant ›Fashion Czar‹ Rudolph Moshammer with his one, his all, his everything, the ›Dog Dame‹ Daisy.

TV-Moderatorin Susann Atwell bei der Präsentation der Diamanten-Robe.

German TV host Susann Atwell during the presentation of the Diamond Robe.

Colours of Dance

Liebe und Verzweiflung, Sehnsucht und Angst, Freude und Schmerz – die verschiedensten Facetten menschlicher Gefühlswelten kommen im Tanz am schönsten zum Ausdruck. Der Tanz spricht die universellste aller Sprachen, denn Emotionen sind global. Unabhängig davon, an was wir glauben, woher wir kommen und wie alt oder jung wir sind: Im Ausdruck des Tanzes entdecken wir uns selbst.

Love and despair, longing and fear, joy and pain – the spectrum of human emotion is most beautifully expressed in the form of dance. Emotions are global and dance is the most universal of languages. Regardless of what we believe, about where we come from, how young or how old we might be, through the expression of dance we discover ourselves.

Colours of Dance: Ein wahrer Rausch der Farben, in dem das ganze Leben mit seinen vielen Facetten tänzerisch dargestellt wird. Eine Erkundungsreise ins Labyrinth unserer Gefühle, zu einem Ort in uns, in dem kulturelle Unterschiede verschmelzen und es eine Sprache gibt, die ohne Worte auskommt.

Colours of Dance is a true rush of colours, where the diversity of life is acted out through dance. It is a dance of discovery through the labyrinth of our emotions to a place within us, where cultural differences melt away and where there is only one language, one which needs no words to be understood.

Choreografiert von Robin Cousins, olympischer Goldmedaillengewinner von 1980 und eine Ikone des Eiskunstlaufs, unterstützt von zahlreichen kreativen Köpfen und dargestellt von den besten Eiskunstläufern, gelingt es *Colours of Dance*, die Zuschauer mit auf die Reise zu nehmen.

Choreographed by the 1980 Olympic gold medalist and figure skating icon Robin Cousins, supported by a team of creative minds and performed by world class skaters *Colours of Dance* takes the audience on a fantastic journey.

Die Reise beginnt in der Großstadt, im Schmelztiegel der verschiedensten Kulturen, wo Hip-Hop und Step-Tanz aufeinander treffen, und führt weiter in eine Tanzschule, in der die verschiedensten Tanzformen der Vergangenheit und der Gegenwart geprobt werden – vom klassischen Ballett bis zum leidenschaftlichen Tango. Feurige Lebenslust, wilde Komik und kühle Eleganz – in der Tanzschule beobachtet eine junge Straßentänzerin die ganze Palette der tänzerischen Bandbreite.

Irgendwann fällt die junge Straßentänzerin in einen tiefen Schlaf – und ihr Traum entführt sie in die Tiefen ihres Unbewussten. Seltsame Szenerien, gefahrvolle Orte, symbolträchtige Arrangements – die Sprache des Unbewussten, tänzerisch umgesetzt, ermutigt den Zuschauer dazu, sein eigenes Labyrinth der Gefühle zu betreten.

Der zweite Akt knüpft dort an, wo der erste aufhört: Der Klang exotischer Musik vertreibt die Traumgespenster, eine Gruppe tibetischer Mönche schwebt herein und zelebriert eine tranceartige Meditation von außergewöhnlicher Schönheit. Die Farben, Formen und die elektrisierende Konzentration der Tänzer – all dies erzeugt einen Eindruck, den niemand so schnell vergessen kann.

It begins in the big city, the cultural melting pot where hip-hop meets step-dancing, and leads to a dance academy where the palette of different dance forms from the past and present are practised - from classical ballet to passionate tango. With a passionate lust for life, wild comedy and cool elegance a young street dancer observes the gamut of dance at the academy.

The young street dancer eventually falls into a deep sleep and her dreams take her to the depths of her unconscious. Strange scenes, dangerous places and symbolic arrangements - the language of the unconscious is set to dance and empowers the audience to enter into their own emotional labyrinth.

The second act picks up where the first leaves off, with the sound of Tibetan music which drives away the dream ghosts. A group of Tibetan monks float into the scene and celebrate a trance like meditation with singular beauty. The colours, forms and the electrifying concentration of the dancers evoke an impression that is unforgettable.

Natürlich darf auch die Liebe nicht zu kurz kommen, hat sie doch die Macht, den Menschen nachhaltig zu bewegen und zu inspirieren. Die Liebe ist das Gefühl, das alle vereint. Wer kennt sie nicht: die Ambivalenz von unendlicher Zartheit und dem alles verschlingenden Magnetismus des Verliebtseins, der gepaart ist mit übermütiger Freude?

Naturally, we also cannot forget about love. Love has the power to move people, to inspire them. Love is the emotion that binds all things together. Who hasn't experienced it? The ambivalence of unending tenderness, the all encompassing magnetism of being in love coupled with unbridled joy!

Der letzte Akt der Show ist zugleich ein neuer Anfang: Die Straßentänzerin kehrt zurück in ihr altes Umfeld. Doch sie ist nicht mehr dieselbe. Viel hat sie erlebt auf ihrer Reise, sie ist reich an Erfahrungen, und sie möchte sie mit anderen teilen. Das große Finale der Show ist ein ausgelassener Tanz mit allen, die ebenso auf der Suche sind wie sie.

The last act of the show is also a new beginning. The streetdancer returns to her old surroundings, but she has changed. She has experienced many new things on her journey and is eager to share the things that she has seen. The show's big finale is a wild group dance with all those who are searching just as she is.

Kostüme
Costumes

Stoffe, Schnitte und Kleider – sie stehen niemals nur für sich selbst, sondern sind immer auch Spiegel und Kommentar ihrer Zeit. Was auf die Mode zutrifft, gilt ebenso für Kostüme – allerdings müssen sich die Kostümdesigner von HOLIDAY ON ICE weiteren Herausforderungen stellen:

Kostüme sollen die Aussage einer Show verstärken und der jeweiligen Szene entsprechen. Sie sollen elegant oder verspielt sein, Sexappeal versprühen oder Glamour ausstrahlen – und dabei immer modern, kreativ und ausdrucksstark bleiben.

Darüber hinaus dürfen die Eiskunstläufer in ihren Bewegungen nicht eingeschränkt werden, auch Sprünge und Hebungen müssen uneingeschränkt ausführbar sein.

Allen Ansprüchen gerecht zu werden, erfordert Weitsicht, Einfühlungsvermögen, Sachverstand und vor allem Kreativität. Perfekte Kostüme sind für eine Show von unschätzbarem Wert. Deshalb arbeitet HOLIDAY ON ICE immer mit den besten Kostümdesignern.

Materials, cuts and clothes – they never stand alone, they are always the reflection and documentation of an era. What is true for clothing goes for costumes as well. But HOLIDAY ON ICE designers have to fulfil other criteria as well.

Costumes should underline the idea of a show or a particular scene. They should be elegant or at times playful, they should exude sex appeal and glamour, at the same time they should be modern and creative while remaining expressive.

Beyond that they should not impede the movement of the skaters, their ability to complete jumps and lifts is an absolute priority.

To fulfil all of these needs requires vision, sensibility, understanding and above all creativity. Perfect costumes for a show are a priceless commodity, therefore HOLIDAY ON ICE always works with the best costume designers in the world.

The three who had the greatest influenence on the ice revue were Billy Livingston, André Levasseur and Folco.

Besonders großen Einfluss auf die Eis-Revue hatten drei von ihnen: Billy Livingston, André Levasseur und Folco.

Billy Livingston entwarf in den 40er und 50er Jahren nicht nur Kostüme für HOLIDAY ON ICE, sondern auch für Sonja Henies Show und ihre Eislauf-Filme. Seine Kostüme waren ihrer Zeit um Jahre voraus und wegweisend für nachfolgende Designer. Acht Jahre lang arbeitete er für diverse Produktionen bei HOLIDAY ON ICE.

André Levasseur, der Lieblingsdesigner von Fürstin Gracia Patricia von Monaco, war ein Multitalent: Er arbeitete nicht nur als Kostüm-, sondern auch als Bühnendesigner. Zwischen 1959 und 1981 entwarf

In the 40's and 50's Billy Livingston not only designed costumes for HOLIDAY ON ICE but also for Sonja Henie's Ice Revue and for her films. His costumes were years ahead of their time and influenced the designers of coming generations. Over the course of 8 years he worked on various HOLIDAY ON ICE productions.

André Levasseur, the favourite designer of Princess Grace of Monaco, was an all around talent. He worked not only as a costume designer but also as a set designer. Between 1959 and 1981 Levasseur designed costumes for 11 HOLIDAY ON ICE productions, each of them stunningly creative.

SKETCH 41
E CUT
HELLA V
SKETCH 42.
CUT
PAT. S.
E
SKETCH 43
SHIRLEY. E
E CUT.
I SUSIE WONG
HEATHER BELBIN.
SKETCH 44
SEQUINNED ALL OVER.
Michael BRONZE '63

Levasseur die Kostüme für 11 Produktionen– alle schillernd vor Einfallsreichtum.

Folco kreierte ab 1958 die Kostüme für sage und schreibe 25 HOLIDAY ON ICE-Produktionen. Er war ein absolutes Ausnahmetalent und für viele der beste Kostümdesigner aller Zeiten. Neben seiner Arbeit für HOLIDAY ON ICE hat Folco 36 Jahre lang die Kostüme für den weltberühmten Lido in Paris entworfen.

Das eleganteste und teuerste Kostüm überhaupt in einer Eis-Revue war eine Kreation von Dior. Für die Grand Dame auf dem Eis – die wunderbare Marika Kilius – entwarf der Pelzdesigner des Hauses, Frédéric Castet, einen weißen Fuchspelz. Das Kostüm für die Abschluss-Szene der *Pink Panther*-Show kostete schon damals – 1977 – ca. 30.000 SFR.

Heute arbeitet HOLIDAY ON ICE mit dem extravaganten Modeschöpfer Rudolph Moshammer zusammen. Der leidenschaftliche HOLIDAY ON ICE-Fan verpasst keine Premiere in seiner Heimatstadt München. Bereits seit seiner Kindheit hegt er eine Vorliebe für das Eislaufen. Seine Entwürfe, darunter eine eisblaue Diamanten-Robe mit Unmengen an Strass und vielleicht einem echten Diamanten, treffen perfekt den Charakter von HOLIDAY ON ICE: höchste Qualität, Sexappeal, Zeitlosigkeit, Glanz und Glamour.

From 1959 onward Folco created costumes for 25 HOLIDAY ON ICE productions! He was a one of a kind talent and for many he was the greatest costume designer of all time. Parallel to his work with HOLIDAY ON ICE Folco designed costumes for the world famous Lido in Paris for 36 years.

The most elegant and expensive costume ever designed for HOLIDAY ON ICE came from Dior. The fur specialist of the house Frédéric Castet, designed a white fox fur for the Grand Dame of the ice, the wonderful Marika Kilius. The costume for the final scene of the *Pink Panther* show cost over 30,000 Swiss Francs in 1977!

Today HOLIDAY ON ICE collaborates with the extravagant fashion designer Rudolph Moshammer. A passionate HOLIDAY ON ICE fan Moshammer never misses a première in his hometown of Munich, and admits that he has had a predilection for figure skating since his childhood. His designs, among them an ice blue diamond robe with countless zircons and perhaps a real diamond or two exemplify the character of HOLIDAY ON ICE, high quality, sex appeal, timelessness, shine and glamour.

FINAL
N° 47
BAUMLER
A.Levasseur

MARIKA
ZAHN-KILIUS

MARIKA
A. Levasseur

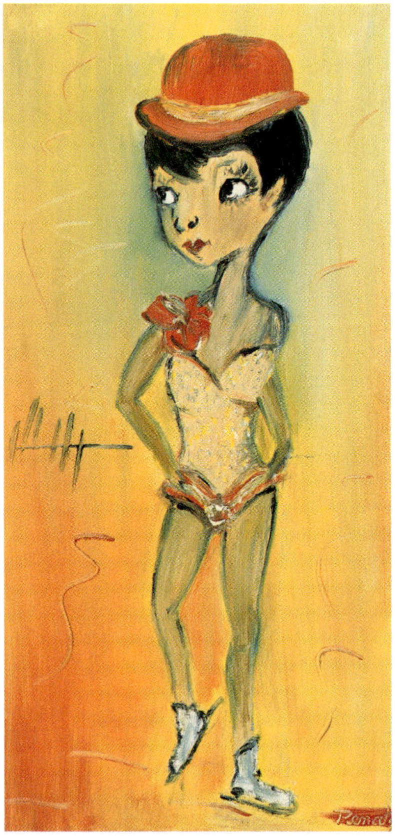

FINAL
SAN FRANCISCO
24 GIRLS
A. Levasseur

C 55 JEWELS
1 SHOW-GIRL

C 52) JEWELS
1 SHOW-GIRL

C 57) JEWELS
1 SHOW-GIRL

C 53) JEWELS
1 SHOW-GIRL

C 56 JEWELS
1 SHOW-GIRL

C 51) JEWELS
1 SHOW-GIRL

Holiday on Ice
opening
12 girls
C 6
(014)
12 GIRLS
OPENING
BROADWAY

Holiday on Ice
Pacific Island
(O 16)

3. 1. (2) solistes

UNIVERCITY
3.1 (3)
ROSELLO

Die Kostüm-Skizzen zur *Hollywood*-Show und ihre Umsetzung auf den folgenden Seiten!

The costume sketches for the *Hollywood* show and their realization on the following pages!

Hollywood

Die Traumfabrik Hollywood mit ihren Stars und Sternchen, mit ihren furiosen Filmen und großen Gefühlen und nicht zuletzt mit ihrer rund 100-jährigen Geschichte – sie gab das Thema bei einer der bezauberndsten HOLIDAY ON ICE-Produktionen vor. Mit dem berühmten Regisseur Anthony van Laast, bekannt durch seine Arbeit mit Andrew Lloyd Webber, und dem Choreografen Robin Cousins, Eiskunstlauf-Olympiasieger von 1980, gelang es HOLIDAY ON ICE auch bei dieser Produktion, hochkarätige Kreative zu verpflichten.

The dream factory Hollywood with its stars and starlets, with its furious films, bombastic emotions and not least of all almost 100 years of history – Hollywood is the theme of one of the most enchanting HOLIDAY ON ICE productions ever made. The success of the show is based on the fact that HOLIDAY ON ICE was able to contract two top notch creative minds for the project: the famous director Anthony van Laast, known through his work with Andrew Lloyd Webber and also the choreographer and olympic gold medal figure skater Robin Cousins.

Wen fesselt sie nicht, die perfekte Unterhaltung, die ein Action-Film bereiten kann – schließlich fasziniert der Kampf zwischen Gut und Böse immer wieder aufs Neue. Gewagte Stunts, schnelle Autos, schöne Frauen und starke Männer – das ist der Stoff, aus dem Action gemacht wird. In *Hollywood* können die Zuschauer live dabei sein, wenn der Held dem Tod ins Auge schaut, um für das Gute einzustehen – und Sie sind live dabei, wenn am Ende als Lohn für überwundene Gefahren die Liebe wartet ...

Who isn't mesmerized by the perfect entertainment that an action film is capable of producing – it seems we never tire of seeing the struggle between good and evil. Dangerous stunts, fast cars, beautiful women and strong men – that is the stuff that action is made of. In *Hollywood* the audience is there live when the hero looks death in the eye, when he stands up for good, and they are also there live when love awaits him as a reward for the dangers that he has overcome.

Als der Schwarz-Weiß-Film gerade von Technicolor abgelöst wurde, waren die Farben entschieden bunter als heute. Die Lippen waren röter, die Wangen rosiger und die Augen blauer. Auch genügten die magischen drei Worte »Ich liebe dich!« um ein 90-köpfiges Orchester auf den Plan zu rufen, die Sonne untergehen zu lassen und den Ruf exotischer Vögel erschallen zu hören. Genießen Sie das Abtauchen in eine Zeit, in der die Frauen von Burt Lancaster und die Männer von Ava Gardner träumten.

When Technicolor replaced black and white films the colours were noticably brighter than today. The lips were 'redder', the cheeks 'rosier' and the eyes were 'bluer'. One only needed to utter those three magical words »I Love You!« for a 90-people orchestra to appear, the sun to go down and the call of exotic birds to resound. Enjoy a trip back in time when women dreamed of Burt Lancaster and men dreamed of Ava Gardner.

Die großen Historienfilme ziehen die Zuschauer auch noch Jahrzehnte nach ihrem Entstehen in den Bann. Aber sind es die Kostüme, die längst vergangene Epochen wieder aufleben lassen, sind es die Requisiten, die an die Pracht versunkener Königreiche erinnern – oder ist es die Musik, die die Spannung ins Unermessliche steigen lässt? Wahrscheinlich ist es alles zusammen – und vor allem sind es die leidenschaftlichen Geschichten und die großen Gefühle, die den Herzschlag der Zuschauer beschleunigen.

The epic historical film still draws fans decades after its advent. Is it the costumes that allow long gone eras to return, or the props that remind us of the wealth of lost kingdoms, or is it the music that drives the tension to unknown heights? It is probably all three and more than that, it is the passionate stories and the momentous emotion that, makes the hearts of the audience race.

Wollten Sie schon immer mal an der Tür lauschen, wenn hoffnungsfrohe junge Talente für eine erste größere Rolle vorsprechen? Wollten Sie schon immer einmal die knisternde Spannung miterleben, wenn große Träume in Erfüllung gehen – oder aber zerplatzen wie Seifenblasen? Bei *Hollywood* erleben Sie live, wie nah und fern zugleich eine Traumrolle sein kann – und wie es sich anfühlt, ein junger talentierter Schauspieler auf der Suche nach Anerkennung

Wouldn't you like to listen through the door when young hopefuls have their first reading? Wouldn't you like to feel the excitement when dreams come true or burst like a bubble? In *Hollywood* you can see live, just how near yet how far a dream role can be. You will feel what it is like to be a talented young actor in search of fame and fortune.

Hollywood entführt sie nicht zuletzt auch in die 80er Jahre – das Jahrzehnt der großen Musikfilme, die die Zuschauer vor Begeisterung aus den Sitzen springen ließen. Erleben sie hautnah die elektrisierende Wirkung der großen dynamischen Choreografien und der explosiven und verträumten Soundtracks, die Jugendliche in Scharen die Kinokassen stürmen ließ und eine Hitsingle nach der anderen an die Spitze der Charts katapultierte.

Hollywood takes you not last of all to the 80's, the decade of music films which had audiences jumping from their seats. Experience the electrifying effect of big, dynamic choreography combined with the explosive and dreamy soundtracks which had kids running to the cinemas in droves to catapult one hit single after another to the top of the charts.

Poster
Posters

Ebenso wie die Kostüme, die Bühnenbilder und die Shows insgesamt dem Wandel der Zeit unterworfen waren, haben sich auch die Plakate deutlich verändert.
War man in den 50er Jahren noch bemüht, alle Szenen einer Show auf dem Plakat zu zeigen, stand in den 70er und 80er Jahren eine Läuferin oder ein Paar stellvertretend für die ganze Show im Vordergrund.

Just as costumes, set designs and the shows themselves have changed over the years, the posters have changed quite a bit too. In the 50's one tried hard to feature every scene from a show, in the 70's and 80's one skater or a couple were featured as a representative for the entire show.

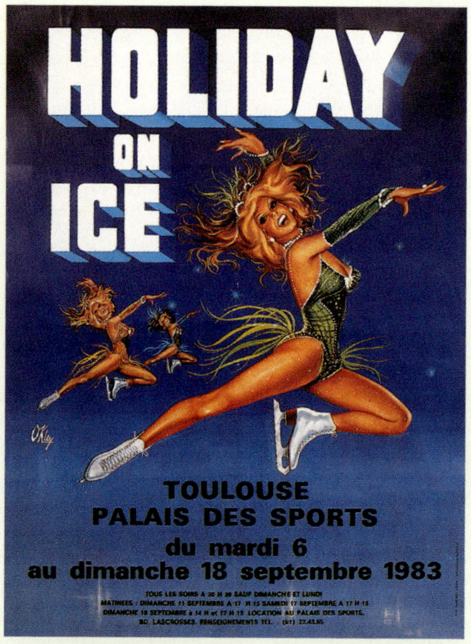

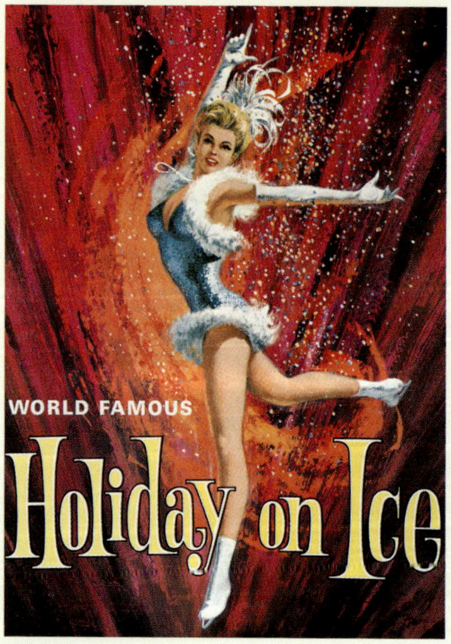

ALL NEW
HOLIDAY ON ICE
of 1952
LAVISH, HILARIOUS GREATER THAN EVER
PACKED WITH BEAUTY, THRILLS COMEDY GALORE
Year's Grandest treat!
with
MICHAEL MEEHAN · JOAN HYLDOFT · GENEVIEVE NORRIS and BOB PAYNE · RUDY RICHARDS · JINX CLARK · LEO FREISINGER · McKELLEN BROS. · PAUL ANDRE · JOAN FREISINGER · PHIL HISER · BOBBY MAY · COUNT RENO · TED MEZA · BILL BLOCKER · FLIP & FLOP · MAY FREISINGER · JACKIE GRANT · CARMEN NAPPO · ARNO BENNETT · JACQUIE HALLQUIST · 36 GLAMOUR-"ICERS". 12 "ICE"-SQUIRES

Ende der 60er und Anfang der 70er Jahre war zwischen einem reich verzierten Schlittschuh und einer Primaballerina alles möglich – gleichbleibend war die Vorliebe für Blumen.

By the end of the 60's and early 70's there was a world of difference between a star studded ice skate and a prima ballerina, the only thing that remained the same was a love of flowers.

SONJA HENIE
dans
sa Revue
HOLIDAY ON ICE 1956

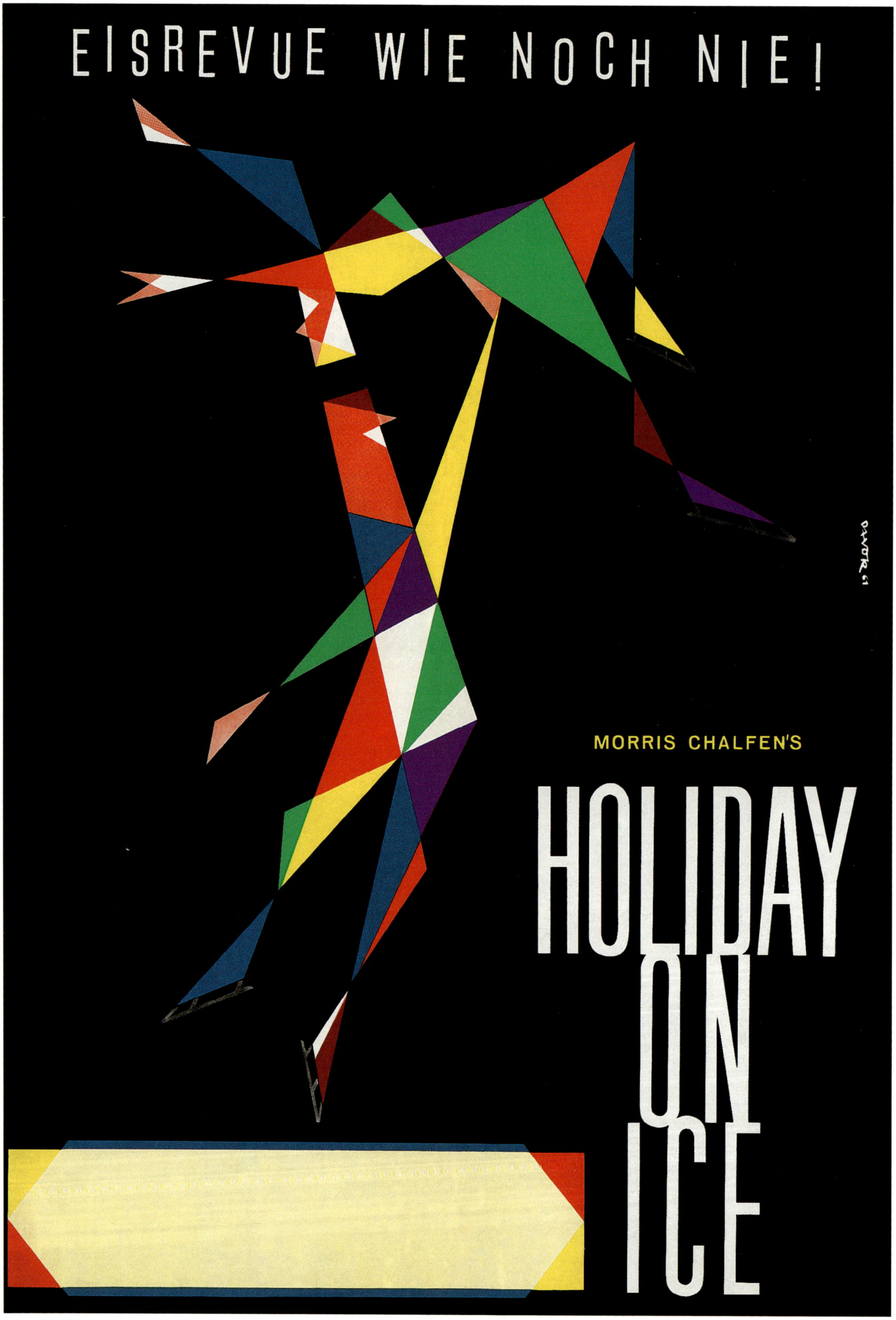
EISREVUE WIE NOCH NIE!
MORRIS CHALFEN'S
HOLIDAY ON ICE

HOLIDAY ON ICE
Magic Show!
POUR LA PREMIERE FOIS AU PALAIS DES SPORTS - PORTE DE VERSAILLES - PARIS
2 MARS
AU
18 AVRIL 93
LES DUCHESNAY
LOCATION
COLLECTIVITES
48 28 50 76

DEUTSCHLANDHALLE
und
Morris Chalfen zeigen:
HOLIDAY
ON ICE
USA
29. Februar
bis
10. März
Täglich 20 Uhr
Mittwochs, sonnabends, und sonntags auch 15 Uhr
Vorverkauf ab 14. Febr. - Eintrittskarten ab 4,- DM, an den Kassen der Deutschlandhalle und den bekannten Vorverkaufsstellen.
Scheck-Nr. 74 (nur gültig für Erwachsene) für 29. Februar, 1. März, 3. März nachmittags und abends, 4. bis 7. März abends.
1968 Druck: Albert Hentrich, 1 Berlin 41, Albrechtstraße 111

HOLIDAY
ON ICE
ALICE NO PAÍS DAS
MARAVILHAS
LEWIS
CAROLLS

HOLIDAY ON ICE

100万ドルの迫力と興奮
MORRIS CHALFEN PRESENTS
SWANLAKE
PRODUCTION
世界プロ・ペアー選手権保持者D.ワトソン・L.カウフマン参加
世界一／アイスショウ団一行90名来日
アメリカン・ホリデイ・オン・アイス
財団法人湯川奨学会基金 9月8日▶10月22日
主催 読売新聞社
協賛 松下電器産業株式会社
後楽園アイスパレス
■入場料／ A 800円 B 600円 (全階指定席)
絶讃前売中／都内各プレイガイド／
■団体のお申込みは (921) 2161 後楽園アイスパレス
(561) 1111 (代 表) 売新聞社企画部
ナショナルステレオ装置

HOLIDAY ON ICE

HOLIDAY ON ICE
Em Maio no
IBIRAPUERA
Guaraná ANTARCTICA
MEU BRASIL BRASILEIRO

HOLIDAY ON ICE 1962
Mittwoch, 15. November bis Sonntag, 3. Dezember 1961
Samstag, 18. und Samstag, 25. November - Samstag, 2. und Sonntag, 3. Dezember auch Nachmittagsvorstellungen 16 Uhr
Volkstrauertag, 19. November - Buß- und Bettag 22. November - Totensonntag 26. November keine Vorstellungen
WESTFALENHALLE

İZMİR BÜYÜKŞEHİR BELEDİYESİ
SANAT ETKİNLİKLERİ
HOLIDAY ON ICE
Buz Revüsü
30 NİSAN - 5 MAYIS
FUAR ATLAS PAVYONU
Bilet Satış Yerleri:
İleri Kitabevi (Konak)
Beymen (Alsancak)
Butik Bravo (Karşıyaka)
Fuar Atlas Pavyonu (Kültürpark)
Biletler numaralıdır 100.000 TL, 75.000 TL.
Bilgi için tel: 21 85 36
Program:
30 Nisan Cuma 21.00
1 Mayıs Cumartesi 17.30
21.00
2 Mayıs Pazar 14.00
17.30
3 Mayıs Pazartesi 21.00
4 Mayıs Salı 21.00
5 Mayıs Çarşamba 17.30
21.00

世界溜冰嘉年華™
HOLIDAY ON ICE™
九龍聖若瑟小學建校籌募會
慈善晚會
聖若瑟英文小學
非賣品

Celebration

Celebration stellt einen Meilenstein in der Geschichte von HOLIDAY ON ICE dar, denn im Verlauf dieser Show durfte die größte Eisrevue der Welt ihren 300-millionsten Besucher begrüßen. Was lag da näher als zu feiern? Diese Idee reifte zu einem Gesamtkonzept für eine Feier des Lebens. *Celebration* präsentiert die vielseitigsten und unterschiedlichsten Ausdrucksformen der Freude und des Feierns mit einer atemberaubenden Geschwindigkeit. Das Publikum wird Zeuge der knisternden Spannung einer Oscar-Verleihung, eines pompösen Wiener Opernballs, eines mondänen Disco-Happenings, ausgelassener Geburtstagspartys und fröhlicher Straßenfeste.

Celebration represents an important milestone in the history of HOLIDAY ON ICE. Because the largest ice skating revue in the world was to greet its 300 millionth visitor during this show! So what could be more appropriate than a party? The idea grew into the overall concept for a festival of life. *Celebration* presents a rich spectrum of expressions of joy and celebration with breathtaking speed. The audience experiences the electrifying tension of Oscar Night, the pomp of the Vienna Opera Ball, a jet set disco party, a carefree birthday party and a happy street party.

Mit der Nacht der Nächte, der festlichen Oscar-Verleihung, beginnt die Vorstellung dieser einzigartigen HOLIDAY ON ICE-Show. Madonnas Hit »Holiday« erweckt das Grand Corps de Ballet mit tosender Partylaune zum Leben – und wenn schließlich zu Daft Punks Song »One more time« die Solisten hinzukommen, wird die Gala-Veranstaltung endgültig zum Dance-Floor.

This one of kind HOLIDAY ON ICE show kicks off with the ›night of nights‹, the Oscars. The Grand Corps de Ballet awakens in a party mood to Madonna's hit »Holiday«, then when the solo stars arrive to the sounds of Daft Punk's »One More Time« the gala event becomes a full-blown dancefloor party.

Traditionsbewusst wird es mit dem Wiener Opernball. Zu Johann Strauss' Morgenzeitungswalzer eröffnet der Zeremonienmeister, ein Herr in eindrucksvoller Abendgarderobe, den traditionellen Ball der Gegenwart. Rauschende Kleider, prächtige Kronleuchter, schöne Frauen und elegante Männer entführen die Zuschauer in die Welt des Debütantinnenballs, die fernab von der schnelllebigen Gegenwart erscheint.

The party is more tradition conscious at the Vienna Opera Ball. Johann Strauss' »Morgenzeitungswalzer« fills the air as the traditional ball is officially opened by the magnificent Master of Ceremonies. Rustling dresses, bombastic chandeliers, beautiful women and elegant men greet the audience as they are introduced into the world of the debutant ball. A world which seems far away from the fast pace of everyday life.

Von der Oper geht es zum Fernsehen. Ein überdimensionaler Bildschirm katapultiert die Zuschauer in die nur scheinbar heile Welt der 50er Jahre. Ein junges Mädchen feiert seinen 18. Geburtstag – doch ihr Freund verschwindet mit einer anderen. Zum Glück hat das Geburtstagskind die richtige Musik zur Hand und lässt sich nicht unterkriegen: »It's my party and I'll cry if I want to« heißt die Zauberformel.

Surreal wird es mit dem Wiesenkäferball. Hier sind Raupen, Käfer und Grashüpfer die Partygäste, und eine kribbelnde und zirpende Fantasiewelt tut sich auf. Wenn schließlich Blumen zu Laternen werden und Pilze in den Himmel wachsen, wird Alice im Wunderland lebendig, und die Augen von Groß und Klein beginnen zu glänzen. Als es plötzlich zu regnen beginnt, suchen zwei kleine Raupen Schutz unter einem goldenen Briefumschlag. Dabei schlafen sie ein und träumen von ihrer Verwandlung in wunderschöne Schmetterlinge. HOLIDAY ON ICE ermöglicht es den Zuschauern mitzuträumen – und lädt sie ein zu einer Reise in den brasilianischen Regenwald ...

From the opera to television. A gigantic television screen catapults the audience into the supposed 'perfect world' of the 1950s. A young girl is celebrating her 18th birthday but then her boyfriend leaves with another girl. Thank goodness the birthday girl has the right music for the occaision, she's not going to let it get her down ... »It's my party and I'll cry if I want to« is the magic antidote.

Things become surreal at the Beetles Ball. Caterpillars, beetles and grasshoppers are the party guests here as a crawling and buzzing world gets swinging. The eyes of young and old light up when Alice in Wonderland comes to life, where flowers become lanterns and mushrooms grow up into the sky. When it suddenly starts to rain two small caterpillars find shelter under a golden envelope. They eventually fall asleep and dream of being transformed into beautiful butterflies. HOLIDAY ON ICE makes it possible for the audience to dream with them and accompany them on a journey through the Brazilian rain forest.

Auch die nächste Szene bleibt in Brasilien, denn ein Fest darf ganz sicher nicht in dem Reigen fehlen: der Karneval von Rio. Rhythmische Samba-Musik erfüllt die Luft, unzählige Menschen tragen farbenfrohe und prächtige Kostüme, riesige Motivwagen fahren auf das Eis – das ist Rio, wie es in der Vorstellung erscheint.

Die Reise geht von Süd- nach Nordamerika – mitten hinein ins Studio 54, den legendären New Yorker Club. Hier verbrachte schon Andy Warhol mondäne Abende. Mit Glitzertreppe, Plateau-Schuhen und riesigen Discokugeln lassen die Solisten und das Grand Corps de Ballet das Flair des legendärsten Clubs aller Zeiten wieder aufleben.

The next scene is also takes place in Brazil. Because there is one party in Brazil that is an absolute must on a 'best of' list and that party is Carnival in Rio! Rhythmic samba music fills the air, crowds of people wearing luxurious, richly colored costumes dance by and parade floats glide across the ice, that's Rio!

The journey continues from South to North America, right into the legendary New York nightclub Studio 54, where Andy Warhol used to spend his evenings with the international jet set. The soloists and the Grand Corps de Ballet use glistening staircases, plattform shoes and an enormous mirrored disco ball to reanimate the spirit of that legendary club.

Bei einer Show wie *Celebration* darf die vielleicht kunstvollste Art zu feiern ganz gewiss nicht fehlen: der Maskenball. Mit aufwändigen Kostümen, faszinierenden Masken und der Musik von Rondo Veneziano findet sich der Zuschauer in der geheimnisvollen Welt Venedigs wieder, die ihren Zauber und ihre Faszination immer wieder aufs Neue unter Beweis stellt.

A show like *Celebration* wouldn't be complete without the artistic costumes of a masquerade ball. Elegant costumes, fascinating masks and the music of »Rondo Veneziano« take the audience to the ever mysterious world of Venice, which reaffirms its magic and excitement again and again.

Rund ums Eis
Totally Ice

Jährlich touren zwischen 3 und 5 HOLIDAY ON ICE-Produktionen durch die ganze Welt. *Diamonds* wird allein im ersten Jahr an 34 verschiedenen Orten zu sehen sein.

Doch wie funktioniert ein Umzug der größten Eis-Revue der Welt? Eines ist sicher: Jeder Standortwechsel ist kostspielig – und die Kosten steigen ständig weiter. Schließlich werden auch die Produktionen immer größer.

Bis zu 25 riesige Container sind mittlerweile nötig, um jegliches Zubehör, sogar die Eisfläche, transportieren zu können.

Every year 3 to 5 HOLIDAY ON ICE productions tour the globe. *Diamonds* alone will be seen in 34 different venues in its first year.

But how does the transport of the largest ice revue in the world actually work? One thing is certain, every change of venue is expensive and costs are constantly rising. The productions themselves are becoming ever bigger.

By now it takes up to 25 large containers to move materials as well as the ice itself from city to city.

Die erste mobile Eismaschine der USA aus den 40er Jahren.

The first mobile ice machine in the USA during the 40's.

Die riesige, noch menschenleere Eishalle zur Weltausstellung in Jakarta 1969.

The giant ice skating arena for the 1969 World's Fair in Jakarta.

So sahen Eispumpen in den 50er Jahren aus.

This is what ice pumps looked like in the 50's.

Sehr viel Platz nimmt natürlich die Bühne ein. Auch wenn jede Bühne bereits in Hinblick auf optimale Transportfähigkeit konstruiert wird, verändern die neuen Technologien den Aufbau stark. Konnte früher eine Bühne über Nacht von Stadt zu Stadt bewegt werden, nehmen Abbau, Transport und Wiederaufbau heutzutage mehr Zeit in Anspruch, denn mittlerweile gehören Video-Projektionsflächen, ferngesteuerte Plattformen und umfangreiche Lichttechnik zum Standard. Hinzu kommt, dass die Bühne auch den speziellen Gegebenheiten wie Größe und Höhe der jeweiligen Hallen angepasst werden muss.

Um möglichst zügig von einer Halle zur anderen wechseln zu können, engagiert HOLIDAY ON ICE zusätzlich zu seinem eigenen Konstruktionsteam Helfer vor Ort.

Auch die durchschnittlich 300 Kostüme reisen von Stadt zu Stadt mit. Um sie kümmern sich 3 bis 4 Garderobieren. Sie säubern, flicken und bügeln die Kostüme wenn nötig auf und bringen verloren gegangene Perlen und Pailletten wieder an den Roben an.

The stage of course takes up a lot of space. Every set is constructed for optimal transportability, however new technologies are drastically altering the construction. In the past a stage could be moved from city to city overnight. Today breakdown, transport and set-up take more time due to the fact that video projection screens, remote control platforms and elaborate lighting systems have become standard equipment. Beyond that, the individual size and height of each arena have to be taken into consideration.

In order to be as quick as possible between venue changes HOLIDAY ON ICE also hires local day labourers in each new city.

An average of 300 costumes are also transported from city to city. Three or four costume specialists are required to take care of them. They clean, repair and iron them as needed and they replace any missing pearls or sequins.

Bleibt noch die für viele spannendste Frage: Wie kommt eigentlich das Eis in die Halle? Ohne die weiße, glitzernde Fläche ist eine Eisrevue schließlich undenkbar.

Der so genannte Eismeister ist eine der wichtigsten Personen hinter den Kulissen und immer als Erster vor Ort.

Circa 72 Stunden dauert es, bis eine Eisfläche beliebiger Größe zur Premiere am Veranstaltungsort nutzbar ist. Selbst tropische Temperaturen sind kein Hindernis. Zuerst wird der Hallenboden mit Styropor und Plastikfolie abgedichtet. Auf diese Schutzschicht kommen etwa 200 Aluminiumplatten, durch die ein mit einem Kühlaggregat verbundenes Röhrensystem verläuft. Holz begrenzt die Ränder, Lücken zwischen den Aluminiumteilen werden mit Sand und Toilettenpapier gefüllt. Stets sind Kreativität und Erfindungsreichtum gefragt.

Nun entsteht das Eis: Wasser ist die erste Deckschicht auf den Aluminiumplatten. Es gefriert, indem Kühlflüssigkeit mit rund minus 13 Grad durch die Röhren in den Platten fließt. Die nächste

Only one question remains, for some the most interesting question. How do they get the ice into the arena? The ice revue is of course inconceivable without its white, glistening surface.

Behind the scenes the so-called ›Ice Master‹ is one of the most important people imaginable and he is always the first person to arrive at each venue.

It takes about 72 hours before an average sized ice surface is ready to be used for a première in a new location. Even tropical temperatures are no problem. First the floor of the arena is covered with styrofoam and sealed with plastic foil. Then roughly 200 aluminum plates with tubes connected to a cooling system running through them are installed. Wood lines the perimeter of the surface, any gaps between the aluminum plates are filled with sand and toilet paper. Creativity and ingenuity are of the essence here!

Now comes the ice. The aluminum plates are covered with water which freezes due to the fact that the coolant flowing through the tubes is about minus 13 degrees Celsius. The next layer is a mix

Schicht, ein Wasser-Kreide-Gemisch, sorgt später für das gleichmäßig strahlend weiße Aussehen der Eisfläche. Ist sie gefroren, trägt der Eismeister weitere Lagen Wasser auf. Der optimale Eisuntergrund für die HOLIDAY ON ICE-Tänzer muss 3 bis 5 Zentimeter dick sein.

Zieht eine Show weiter, wird das Eis auf minus 30 Grad gekühlt, so wird es brüchig und lässt sich entsorgen. Die Kühlflüssigkeit wird zurück in ihren dafür vorgesehenen Tankcontainer gepumpt – und die Reise kann weitergehen.

of water and chalk which makes the even, white shimmer of the ice possible. Once this freezes the ›Ice Master‹ puts down several more layers of water. The optimal ice surface for a HOLIDAY ON ICE dancer has to be between 3 to 5 centimeters thick.

When the show moves on the ice is cooled to minus 30 degrees where it becomes brittle and is easy to dispose of. The coolant is pumped back into its transport tank and the show rolls on.

Evolution

Was gibt es Spannenderes als die Geschichte der Zivilisation? *Evolution* lädt die Zuschauer ein zu einer turbulenten Zeitreise durch die Vergangenheit – und ist nichts weniger als ein Festival des Lebens, das die Magie und die Wunder der Welt samt der Schönheit der Kultur beschreibt. Verschiedene getanzte Szenen, die ihre Faszination aus der Harmonie des Eiskunstlaufs und der schöpferischen Kraft des jungen belgischen Choreografen Francis Demarteau beziehen, spannen den Zeitbogen von der aufregenden Geburtsstunde des Universums bis hinein in eine ferne Zukunft.

What cold be more exciting than the history of civilization? *Evolution* takes the audience on a turbulent journey through time, into the past. *Evolution* is nothing less than a festival of life which describes the magic and miracle of the world along with the beauty of culture. The harmony of figure skating and the creative talents of the young Belgian choreographer Francis Demarteau are combined in a fascinating variety of dance scenes which cover the spectrum of time from the beginnings of the universe into the near future.

Womit sollte *Evolution* sonst beginnen, als mit der Ur- und Frühgeschichte unseres Planeten? Tänzerisch entsteht aus dem Chaos der Schöpfung eine neue Welt. Voller Freude begrüßt der Mensch das Aufgehen der Sonne, die alles Leben erschafft. Im Idyll der ursprünglichen Landschaft jagen währenddessen wilde Tiere – sie kämpfen um ihre Existenz.

Ein bisschen Spaß muss sein – und was gibt es bei diesem Thema Passenderes als den Zusammenprall einer Ameisenschar mit einem waschechten Dinosaurier? Das heillose Durcheinander, das mit vierundzwanzig Ameisen und einem Dinosaurier entsteht, muss Jung und Alt zum Lachen bringen.

Kaum hat sich eine Form von Ordnung etabliert, gerät diese schon wieder in Gefahr – diesmal durch die Barbaren. Brüllend, kettenrasselnd und zerstörend rauschen sie wie eine Flutwelle über das Eis, um die bestehende Ordnung ins Chaos zu stürzen.

Where else could the story of *Evolution* start than with the birth and beginnings of our own prehistoric planet. The dance shows a new world emerge from the chaos of creation. Man, full of joy, greets the rising sun which creates all life. Wild animals roam through the prehistoric idyll, fighting for their own survival.

But we have to have a little fun too! And what could be funnier than a real dinosaur confronted with an army of ants? The slapstick that occurs when twenty-four ants meet a dinosaur has young and old laughing out loud.

Order has barely been established when it is put in grave danger - by the barbarians! Howling, chain wielding and destructive, they rush across the ice like a tidal wave to cast order back into chaos.

Weiter führt die Zeitreise ins alte Ägypten. Die mythenumrankte, schöne Kleopatra steigt zusammen mit ihrem Pharao in prunkvoller Kleidung in den Tempel des Sonnengotts. Ekstatische Spannung macht sich breit, als sich der jahrtausendealte Sarkophag öffnet und ihm die strahlende göttliche Schönheit entsteigt.

Our journey then leads us to ancient Egypt. The mysterious and beautiful Cleopatra, in stunning costume, enters the temple of the sun god with her Pharaoh. An ecstatic tension fills the air as the thousand-year-old sarcophagus opens and the radiant godly beauty steps out.

Wieder gibt es einen Zeitsprung von mehreren tausend Jahren – mitten hinein in die Wiener Romantik. Der Zuschauer erlebt hautnah die Mystik und Magie der Wiener Atmosphäre des 18. Jahrhunderts, als ein Wunderknabe namens Mozart und ein Komponist namens Beethoven die Metropole mit dem berühmten Schmäh weltbekannt machten.

Again we travel several thousand years into the future, into the Viennese romantic era. The audience experiences first hand the mystery and magic of eighteenth century Vienna. Where a child prodigy by the name of Mozart and a composer by the name of Beethoven are making the city with the notoriously funny accent world famous.

Kleidung und Mode waren schon immer Teil der Kultur und der Zivilisation – ein Grund mehr, sich der faszinierenden Welt der Haute Couture zu widmen! Eine traumhafte Modenschau, live auf dem Eis, lässt die Faszination und den Glamour der Welt des schönen Scheins auferstehen.

Nach einer Hommage an die verrückten Siebziger mit Flowerpower und Schlaghosen sowie einem Ballett der Flammen als Huldigung an die Kraft des Feuers und seiner immensen Bedeutung für alle Kulturen, wird der Bogen in die Zukunft gespannt: »Metropolis« heißt die Szene, die mit fantastischen Kostümen die albtraumhafte Vision von alles beherrschenden Maschinen beschreibt.

Clothing and fashion have always been a part of culture and civilization, just one more reason to devote a special tribute to the fascinating world of Haute Couture! A dreamy fashion show, live on the ice resurrects the fascinating and glamourous world of beauty and appearances.

After an hommage to the crazy 70's complete with flowerpower and bell bottoms as well as a ›Ballet of Flames‹, a worshiping of the power of fire and its enormous importance to all cultures, a leap into the future takes place. »Metropolis« is the name of the final scene of the show in which the nightmarish vision of a world controlled by machines is acted out in fantastic costumes.

Auf Reisen
On Tour

HOLIDAY ON ICE ist überall zu Hause, in mehr als 80 Ländern auf allen 5 Kontinenten. 1943 in den USA ins Leben gerufen, gastierte die Show bereits 1947 zum ersten Mal in Mexico City. 1949 folgte die erste Südamerika-Tournee, und 1950 ging es nach Europa.

Was in Brüssel gar nicht so viel versprechend begann, änderte sich rasch. Schon Anfang der 50er Jahre kannte man HOLIDAY ON ICE in ganz Europa: Angefangen in Spanien, wo die Show in riesigen Stierkampfarenen gastierte, tourte HOLIDAY durch Portugal, Frankreich, die Schweiz, Belgien und Skandinavien bis nach Italien. In Deutschland eroberten Ria Baran und Paul Falk bei ihrem Auftritt in der Dortmunder Westfalenhalle die Herzen der Zuschauer im Sturm.

Etwa zur gleichen Zeit trat eine separate HOLIDAY ON ICE-Show in Südamerika auf, eine andere Truppe feierte 1953 in Tokio Japan-Premiere.

HOLIDAY ON ICE is at home around the world, in more than 80 countries and on all 5 continents. After starting in America in 1943, the show was already playing in Mexico City by 1947. The first South American tour followed in 1949 and in 1950 it was off to Europe.

Though prospects looked bleak in Brussels, things were about to change fast. By the beginning of the 50's HOLIDAY ON ICE was known throughout Europe. Starting in Spain where shows took place in enormous bull fighting arenas, HOLIDAY went to Portugal, France, Switzerland, Belgium, Scandanavia and Italy. In Germany Ria Baran and Paul Falk won the hearts of the audience during their performances at the Dortmunder Westfalenhalle.

Around the same time a separate HOLIDAY ON ICE show toured South America and another troupe celebrated its Japanese première in 1953.

1955 hatte sich HOLIDAY ON ICE auf vier Kontinenten etabliert – und ein Jahr später konnte Sonja Henie das größte Hallenstadion der westlichen Erdhalbkugel in Rio de Janeiro eröffnen. 1958 durfte HOLIDAY ON ICE die Vereinigten Staaten sogar auf der Expo in Brüssel vertreten. Bald darauf suchte sich Geschäftsführer Morris Chalfen eine neue Herausforderung und leistete weitere Pionierarbeit: Er wollte HOLIDAY ON ICE als erste amerikanische Attraktion in der damaligen Sowjetunion etablieren. Chalfen gelang es, das US-Außenministerium zu überzeugen, und so stand seinem Vorhaben nichts mehr im Wege. Im Zuge des zwischen den beiden Supermächten neu vereinbarten Kulturaustauschs hatte HOLIDAY ON ICE im Frühling 1959 seinen ersten Gastauftritt in Moskau – vor ausverkauftem Haus. Dies sollte sich auch weitere acht Wochen lang nicht ändern.

Nach dem großen Erfolg in Moskau war das amerikanische Außenministerium sehr darauf bedacht,

By 1955 HOLIDAY ON ICE was firmly established on four continents. One year later Sonja Henie would open the largest indoor arena in the western hemisphere in Rio de Janiero. In 1958 HOLIDAY ON ICE represented the USA at the World's Fair in Brussels. Shortly thereafter HOLIDAY ON ICE manager Morris Chalfen went all out in looking for new challenges. He was intent on establishing HOLIDAY ON ICE as the first American attraction to travel to the Soviet Union. Chalfen convinced the US State Department of the idea and then nothing could stop him. In the spring of 1959 HOLIDAY ON ICE played to a sold out house in Moscow as part of a newly established cultural exchange programme between the superpowers. The show sold out for eight more weeks.

After its huge success in Moscow, the US State Department was keen on presenting HOLIDAY ON ICE in the developing countries of Africa, as the

Auf nach Graceland! Elvis Presley war zu seiner Zeit als GI in Frankfurt ein häufiger Gast bei HOLIDAY ON ICE. Als er in die USA zurückgekehrt war und HOLIDAY gerade Gastauftritte in Memphis bestritt, lud er das gesamte Ensemble in sein Haus ein.

We 're off to Graceland! As a GI in Frankfurt, Elvis Presley was a regular guest of HOLIDAY ON ICE. After returning to America he invited the entire HOLIDAY ensemble to pay a visit during their stop in Memphis.

HOLIDAY ON ICE in den sich neu entwickelnden Staaten Afrikas zu präsentieren – schließlich rangen Amerikaner und Russen um möglichst viel Einfluss auf diese Länder.

Der Tournee-Auftakt fand in Kartoum im Sudan statt. Es folgten Auftritte in Kenia, Uganda, Tansania, Mozambique, Nyasaland (heute Malawi) und Sambia. An der afrikanischen Westküste stand zunächst Louanda in Angola auf dem Spielplan. Nach dem Engagement in der nigerianischen Stadt Lagos präsentierte sich HOLIDAY ON ICE in dem kleinen Dorf Enugu. Im Frühling und Frühsommer 1960 tourte eine andere Gruppe in Nordafrika mit Gastspielen in Casablanca (Marokko), Tunis (Tunesien) und Tripolis (Libyen).

Einfach waren diese Reisen nicht, manche Umstände ließen einen Auftritt schier unmöglich erscheinen. Doch HOLIDAY ON ICE trotzte allen Widrigkeiten.

Americans and the Russians were engaged in a heated battle to win influence there.

The tour kicked off in Karthoum, Sudan. Shows in Kenya, Uganda, Tanzania, Mozambique, Nyasaland (today Malawi) and Zambia followed. After performing in the Nigerian city of Lagos HOLIDAY ON ICE played in the tiny village of Enungu. During the spring and summer of 1960 another troupe toured North Africa with appearances in Casablanca (Morocco), Tunis (Tunesia) and Tripoli (Lybia). It was no easy trip and at times performances seemed as though they would be impossible, but HOLIDAY ON ICE met every challenge.

In 1964 Prague was on the schedule for the first time, from there the show moved on to St. Petersburg (Leningrad at the time) and returned to Moscow.

新明星！新節目！新設備！新姿態！

南方晚報

NANFANG EVENING POST

新嘉坡羅敏申律四十五號

PRINTED AND PUBLISHED AT 45, ROBINSON ROAD, SINGAPORE 1.

P. O. BOX NO. 37

Saturday July 2 1955 (定價角半) 星期六 一九五五年七月二日

一九五五

白雪溜冰團

團員廿人包括十九個國籍

Selbstverständlich gab es auch rund um den Erdball immer wieder hohen Besuch bei den Shows.

Distinguished guests were a common sight at HOLIDAY ON ICE performances around the world.

1964 schließlich stand erstmals Prag auf dem Spielplan der Show. Von dort ging es erneut nach St. Petersburg, damals Leningrad, und Moskau.

Auch in den 60er Jahren expandierte HOLIDAY ON ICE – jetzt allerdings hauptsächlich im Ursprungsland USA und in Kanada. Über die Gastspiele in den bereits bekannten Städten wie Cincinatti, Indianapolis und Milwaukee hinaus gab es Auftritte in Toronto, Oakland, San Francisco, San Diego und Los Angeles. Die Hauptarena war zweifellos der Madison Square Garden in New York – 1965 konnte HOLIDAY ON ICE das Publikum dort mit einer Star-Besetzung, bestehend aus Ronnie Robertson, Sjoukje Dijkstra sowie Eva und Pavel Roman, für sich gewinnen. Und noch etwas anderes geschah 1965: Mit der Verpflichtung von Marika Kilius und Hans-Jürgen Bäumler hielt es die deutschen Zuschauer bei HOLIDAY ON ICE nicht mehr auf den Sitzen. Bei nahezu jeder Vorstellung gab es Standing Ovations für das deutsche Traumpaar.

Ebenfalls 1965 gab es zudem zum ersten Mal eine Show in Israel – auch hier spielte das Team vor komplett ausverkauftem Haus.

Die 70er und 80er Jahre waren stark von Expansion geprägt. Rund um den Globus wurden neue, riesige Arenen errichtet. Um sie alle bespielen zu können, unterhielt HOLIDAY ON ICE zu dieser Zeit 6 Truppen.

Erneut ging es in die ehemalige UDSSR – zum dritten Mal. Auch in die damalige DDR zog es HOLIDAY ON ICE: Anlässlich der 750-Jahrfeier Ost-Berlins 1987 gab die Show mit 27 ausverkauften Vorstellungen im Friedrichstadt-Palast ihr Debüt. Weitere Vorstellungen folgten in Karl-Marx-Stadt (heute Chemnitz), Halle und Dresden.

Auch in der jüngsten Vergangenheit gab es immer wieder Ereignisse, die aus dem bewegten Leben der Eisrevue herausstechen: 1999 zeigten HOLIDAYs Stars ihre Virtuosität unter freiem Himmel auf dem Amsterdamer Uitmarkt. Die 30-minütige Aufführung wurde live im niederländischen Fernsehen übertragen, und die Resonanz vor Ort und vor dem Bildschirm war überwältigend.

Heute, nach einer 60-jährigen Geschichte, kann HOLIDAY ON ICE auf rund 90.000 Vorstellungen in mehr als 650 verschiedenen Städten und mehr als 80 Ländern zurückblicken – eine imposante Zwischenbilanz.

HOLIDAY ON ICE expanded further in the 60's for the most part in its home of North America. Beyond performances in established venues such as Cincinnati, Indianapolis and Milwaukee the cities of Toronto, Oakland, San Francisco, San Diego and Los Angeles were added. The main arena was without a doubt Madison Square Garden in New York. In 1965 HOLIDAY ON ICE thrilled crowds with a star studded cast including Ronnie Robertson and Sjoukje Dijkstra as well as the sister/brother pair Eva and Pavel Roman. After signing the pair of Marika Kilius and Hans-Jürgen Bäumler in 1965 there was no way of keeping German audiences in their seats. The German dream pair received standing ovations after nearly every performance.

In 1965 HOLIDAY ON ICE played in Israel for the first time, and they played to a sold out crowd.

In the 70's and 80's the expansion continued. Enormous new arenas were being built around the world and in order to play them HOLIDAY ON ICE maintained six touring groups.

Once again HOLIDAY ON ICE returned to the Soviet Union for a third time and then they went on to East Germany. To celebrate the 750th anniversary festivities in East Berlin in 1987 HOLIDAY's debut played 27 sold out shows at the Friedrichstadt Palast. More shows followed in Karl Marx Stadt (now Chemnitz), Halle and Dresden.

The recent past has also been full of events which stand out in the long life of the ice revue, such as the Uitmarkt performance in the middle of Amsterdam. In 1999 the Uitmarkt in Amsterdam offered HOLIDAY ON ICE a wonderful opportunity to show off the virtuosity of its stars in a 30-minute open air show. The show was broadcast live on Dutch television and the excitement of the audience both at home and at the Uitmarkt was phenomenal.

Today 60 years of HOLIDAY ON ICE can look back on more than 90,000 performances, in 650 cities, in more than 85 countries - pretty impressive for an interim balance.

Xotika

Xotika entführt in die Tiefen des Herzens. Es ist eine Reise auf der Suche nach Liebe, eine Reise ins Land der Magie und der Mystik. Stellvertretend für uns bricht ein Held auf, lässt sein Zuhause zurück, besteht gefährliche Abenteuer, erwehrt sich unheimlicher Trugbilder, taucht ab in ein geheimnisvolles Land, an unbekannte Orte, zu unbekannten Wesen.
Aber er verliert nie sein Ziel aus den Augen: die Suche nach Liebe und Erfüllung. Die Suche nach Xotika.

Xotika takes us to the depths of the heart. It is a journey in search of love, a journey to a land of magic and mysticism. A hero embarks on a journey on our behalf. He leaves his home behind, survives dangerous adventures, fights off eerie hallucinations and descends into a land of magic, to unknown places and unknown beings. Along the way he never loses sight of his goal, the search for love and fulfilment, the search for Xotika.

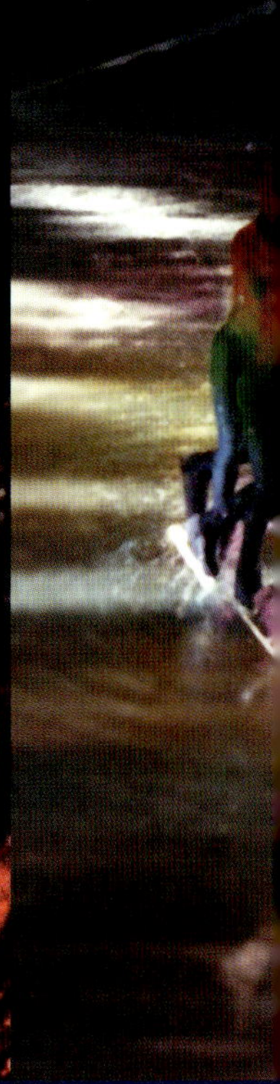

Mit einer fantastischen Choreografie, farbenprächtigen Kostümen, einer brillanten Musik und jeder Menge Kreativität und Talent gelingt es dem Team, die Zuschauer in eine Welt zu entführen, die Traumland und Sehnsucht in einem ist.

Noch ist der Held zu Hause in seiner Unterwasserwelt. Mit Hilfe eines Amuletts macht er sich von dort aus auf den Weg. Aus dem Unterwasserparadies aufgetaucht, führt ihn die Reise zuerst an einen Strand. Hier pulsiert das pralle Leben: Die Farben sind bunter und die Stimmen lauter, es gibt Jongleure und Hula-Hoop-Tänze, bis die Sonne im Meer versinkt. Aber Xotika findet er hier nicht.

By combining fantastic choreography, unbelievable costumes and brilliant music with loads of creativity and talent the HOLIDAY ON ICE team is able to take the audience to a place where dreams and desire become one.

The story begins with our hero at home in an underwater world. With the help of a magical amulette he embarks upon his journey. Leaving the underwater paradise his journey takes him to a beach. The beach is pulsing, full of life; colours are brighter, voices are louder, there are jugglers juggling and hoola-hoop dancers dancing until the sun sinks into the ocean. But Xotika is nowhere to be found.

Die zweite Station ist die Wüste. Dort durchlebt der Held Momente wilder Leidenschaft und tödlicher Gefahr – doch mit Hilfe seines Amuletts besteht er die Prüfungen und kann seine Reise fortsetzen. Sie führt ihn schließlich zum Baum des Lebens in den Garten der Unschuld, wo er der Versuchung nicht widerstehen kann: Er nascht von den verbotenen Früchten, verliert seine Unschuld und taucht ein in eine Welt von Liebe und Lust.

Der Weg führt weiter in die Welt der Mythen und Symbole. Zyklopen tauchen auf und Larven. Sie spinnen ihn ein und stehlen ihm sein Amulett. Was soll er nun tun? Bevor ihn weiteres Unglück ereilt, flieht er zu den Elementen Wind und Erde.

The second stop of the journey is the desert. Here our hero survives moments of unbridled passion and life threatening danger, with the help of his amulette he masters these tests and continues along on his journey. He is eventually led to the tree of life in the Garden of Innocence where he is unable to resist temptation ... he partakes from the forbidden fruit, loses his innocence and is transported into a world of love and lust.

The path leads further into a world of myths and symbols. Cyclopses appear, as well as larvae. They tie him up in a cocoon and steal his amulette. What can he do now? Before more bad luck descends upon him he calls to the elements of wind and earth for help.

Unterstützt von den beiden elementaren Gewalten gelingt es unserem Helden, sein Amulett mit den magischen Fähigkeiten wiederzuerlangen. Erneut spürt er Lebensfreude und Tatendrang und kann sich wieder auf die Suche machen – auf die Suche nach Xotika.

Supported by the two elementary powers our hero is able to recapture his magic amulette. Renewed with a joy for life and a thirst for action he can resume his search – the search for Xotika.

Schließlich gelangt er an den Fuß eines Berges: Findet er Xotika hier? Sirenenhaft hört er Xotikas Echo überall und verliert darüber fast den Verstand. Aber auch hier bleibt er erfolglos.

Finally he approaches the base of a mountain, will he find Xotika here? He hears Xotika's echo everywhere, the siren's call disorients him to the point of insanity. Still he remains unsuccessful.

Er muss weitersuchen – zunächst auf einem Tango-Ball. Der leidenschaftliche Tango – ist er Xotika? Nein, denn nach weiteren Stationen, die der Held auf sich nehmen muss, nach Abenteuern, die ihn in große Gefahr bringen und nach einem langen Weg voller Irrungen und Wirrungen begreift er: Xotika ist in ihm selbst, Xotika ist in jedem von uns.

He must go on, next to a tango ball. The passionate tango – is this Xotika? No, because after further stations and more dangerous adventures, after a long journey full of disorientation and illusion he realizes, Xotika is in him, Xotika is in every one of us.

Danksagungen
Acknowledgements

Unser besonderer Dank gilt allen Personen, die in außergewöhnlicher Weise zu Inhalt und Entstehung dieses Jubiläumsbandes zum 60-jährigen Bestehen von HOLIDAY ON ICE beigetragen haben:

José Kerkoerle, dem ehemaligen Chief Executive Officer von HOLIDAY ON ICE

Robin Cousins, dem Olympiasieger im Eiskunstlauf von 1980 und derzeitigen Creative Director und Choreografen verschiedener HOLIDAY ON ICE-Shows

Peter O'Keeffe, dem Executive Producer von HOLIDAY ON ICE

Jolijn Venema, der Assistentin im Communications Department von HOLIDAY ON ICE

Gritt Rödiger, der PR-Managerin von HOLIDAY ON ICE in Deutschland

und nicht zuletzt dem gesamten Team der Egmont vgs verlagsgesellschaft.

We would like to give special thanks to all those who have contributed in exceptional ways to the content and creation of this book celebrating 60 years of HOLIDAY ON ICE productions:

José Kerkoerle, former Chief Executive Officer of HOLIDAY ON ICE Productions

Robin Cousins, 1980 Olympic Skating Champion, now Creative Director and Choreographer of various HOLIDAY ON ICE shows

Peter O'Keeffe, Executive Producer of HOLIDAY ON ICE Productions

Jolijn Venema, Assistant to the Communications Department of HOLIDAY ON ICE Productions

Gritt Rödiger, PR Manager of HOLIDAY ON ICE in Germany

and last but not least the whole team of the Egmont vgs verlagsgesellschaft.

Ruud Steenhuisen

Geschäftsführer von HOLIDAY ON ICE in Deutschland

Managing Director of HOLIDAY ON ICE in Germany

Morris Chalfen presents
WORLD FAMOUS
HOLIDAY ON ICE

Impressum
Imprint

Die Deutsche Bibliothek – CIP-Einheitsaufnahme

Bibliografische Information Der Deutschen Bibliothek

Die Deutsche Bibliothek verzeichnet diese Publikation in der Deutschen Nationalbibliografie; detaillierte bibliografische Daten sind im Internet über

http://dnb.ddb.de abrufbar.

Das Buch von Natalia Ewakowa, übersetzt von Jon Shelton, entstand zum 60-jährigen Jubiläum von Holiday On Ice

1. Auflage 2003

Redaktion: Petra Flocke

Lektorat: Katharina Schwarze

Produktion: Susanne Beeh

Umschlaggestaltung, Layout und Satz: Metzgerei Strzelecki, Köln

Bildnachweis: © dpa/Frankfurt für folgende Abbildungen: S. 24 Baran/Falk; S. 27 Eigel; S. 34 Kilius/Bäumler; S. 38 Candeloro; S. 39 Vlachtchenko; S. 39 Anissina/Peizerat

Alle weiteren Abbildungen: © Holiday on Ice

Druck: Appl, Wemding

Printed in Germany

ISBN 3-8025-3286-4

Besuchen Sie auch unsere Homepages:

www.vgs.de

www.holidayonice.com